DPH SPORTS SERIES

SNOOKER AND BILLIARDS

Ashok Kumar

DISCOVERY PUBLISHING HOUSE
New Delhi-110002

First Published-1999
Reprint 2006

ISBN 81-7141-475-3

Published by:
DISCOVERY PUBLISHING HOUSE
4831/24, Ansari Road, Prahlad Street,
Daryaganj, New Delhi-110 002 (*INDIA*)
Phone: 3279245
Fax: 91-11-3253475

Printed at:

Tarun Offset Printers, Delhi-53

PREFACE

The need of having a sports series felt because today's situation of the world is not conducive to peace, all round there is destruction, despair, conflict and war; war if not between two nations then within the country itself. In a world where there are some 820 million people unemployed or under-employed, and where 86 million people are born every year, it is not surprising that one out of every four individuals lives in absolute poverty. The *Discovery Publishing House* by Publishing this series seeks to get positive response as—to means by which sports can promote and propagate peace and international cooperation. Sportsmen form a large identifiable cadre. We visualises a situation where a conscious efforts is made all over the world to train the sportspersons to spread the message of peace and international cooperation. Instead of peace keeping efforts through arms and army, the sportspersons may be used as soldiers of peace in a subtle manner. The effort is to make the realize the contribution of sports as a factor for sustainable development, peace keeping and international cooperation.

In developing countries, sports development cooperation is still in the need of justification and steadfast arguments. Many people ask the question "why invest in sports in developing countries for which water supply, health service and agriculture projects are much better suited? An apt reply to this question may be "for many of the people of a developing country,

Sports is the only 'Sweaty' Leisure-time activity. Sports represents a moment of joy in the midst of hard poverty-stricken and dirty everyday life. Doing sports even makes one's work go more smoothly the next day.

This series will be useful to the sports promoters, organisers, coaches and other persons related or interested in sports.

Editor

CONTENTS

1

INTRODUCTION

Pyramids, perhaps snooker's most obvious forerunner, was a game played with 15 reds, initially placed in a triangle, with the apex red on what Is now the pink spot but which was then known as the pyramid spot. Each time a player potted a red, all his opponents paid across the agreed stake money per ball. In life pool, each player was given a cue-ball and an object-ball so, for the second player, his object-ball was the first player's cue-ball and so on. The object was to pot one's specified object-ball three times. Each time a player's ball was potted, he lost a life and had to pay an agreed stake. When he had lost three "lives" he paid an extra sum for a "star" and when that was gone he was "dead". When only one player remained he scooped the kitty.

Black pool was a development of pool in that a black ball was added. When a player had potted his allocated ball, he could attempt the black. If he was successful, each of his opponents paid across an additional sum and he could then attempt the nearest ball. Joe Davis spent many of his youthful hours playing a similar game, pink pool. Black pool was the preferred game among the Devonshire officers but it was Chamberlain's inspiration gradually to add other coloured balls so that snooker came to be played with 15 reds, yellow, green pink and black. Blue and brown were added so years later. These new colours produced a game whose variety immediately caught on. The concept of break-building was much in the future and even the point values the balls were not established until a little later; but was in these casual and almost chance beginnings that the game undoubtedly had its origins. When Compton Mackenzie, the novelist, interviewed him in 1938, Chamberlain recalled that the Devons one afternoon received a visit from a you subaltern who had been trained at the Royal Military Academy, Woolwich. In the course of conversation the latter happened to remark that a first-year cadet Woolwich was referred to as a "snooker" with the implication that this was the status of the lowest of the low. The original word for a cadet had been the French "neux" which had been corrupted "snooker".

Chamberlain said: "The term was a new one to me but I soon had the opportunity of exploiting it when one of our party failed to hole ' a coloured ball which was close to a corner pocket. I called out to hi 'Why, you're a regular snooker.' "I had to explain to the company the definition the word and to soothe the feelings of the culprit added that we were all, so to speak, snookers at the game so it would be very appropriate to call the gain snooker. The suggestion was adopted with et thuslasm and the game has been called snooker ever since."

In 1876, when Chamberlain left the Devons to join the Central India Horse, he took the game with him. After being wounded in the Afghan war, he served with the commander-in-chief of the Madras army and was with him every summer when he moved to the hill station at Ootacamund. Snooker came to be recognised as the speciality of the Ooty Club and the rules of the game were drawn up and posted in the billiards room.

During the 1880s rumours of this new game reached England and when John Roberts went to India on one of his tours he had it in his mind to find out the rules. One evening in 1885 in Calcutta, Chamberlain was dining with the Maharajah of Cooch Behar when Roberts was introduced to him. Roberts duly brought the game back to England. It was many a long day before snooker became widely played. Not every hall nor every club could afford a snooker set of 22 balls though it was not long before the manufacturers appreciated snooker's superior commercial possibilities.

As far as competition was concerned there was nothing until 1916 when Harry Hardy, owner of Hoprend, Hopsack and other winners of the Waterloo Cup, suggested an amateur snooker championship. The standard was poor and in 1918, in fact, an American, H.H. Lukens, won the championship after only a few weeks' practice at the Palmerston Restaurant, under the pseudonym of T.N. Palmer.

The rules of snooker, which had been subject to many local variations, were codified when the Billilards Association and Billiards Control Club amalgamated in 1919. The drawn game was abolished when provision was made for the black to be re-spotted at the end of a frame if the scores were equal. The free ball was introduced, but the penalty for going in-off a red was still only one, the four-point minimum penalty being a few years away. Low as the standard was in the amateur championship, it was not long before the provincial players, nurtured in money games, elbowed the more "gentlemanly" type of entrant to one side, though not before Sidney Fry, in 1919, had become the first to accomplish the billiards-snooker amateur championship double, a feat he was within a ball of repeating in 1921 when he had a shot at the black in the final before losing to M.J. Vaughan.

The seven-frame final was decided then, as it was until 1927, on aggregate score. The change was precipitated, after several years' rumbling, by the 1926 final in which W. Nash beat F.T.W. Morley, who entered under the name of his stepfather, Leaphard, 383-356, though Morley won four of the seven frames. Jack McGlynn, at different times of both Birmingham and Nottingham, won the title twice around this period, as did Walter Coupe. Play was largely of a tactical nature, a red, a colour and safety being the order of the day. Breaks of 27 by McGlynn and W.E. Foster were the best up to 1925 when the record shot up dramatically to 62 through W.L. Crompton.

In 1927, the year the touching ball rule was introduced, Ollie Jackson, a safety expert whose top break in the championship was 38, won the title but did not defend in 1928 when Pat Matthews, a 23-year-old watchmaker who attributed his success to a fruit diet., principally prunes, beat Frank Whittall 54, on the final black, to record the first of his four titles.

There were a few professional matches in the 1920s: Fred Lawrence beat Albert Cope 3127 for the Midland professional championship in 1921; J.S.

Nicholls beat W. Davies 1,032-777 for the Welsh professional championship in 1922; and R.S. Williams made a break of 81 in South Africa, where snooker was reported to be very popular.

Snooker was chiefly a gambling game or a respite from billiards, but the Billiards Professionals Association, an organisation for markers and professionals attached to clubs rather than the big names of the day, organised a snooker tournament in 1923 in which Tom Dennis, who owned a billiard hall in Nottingham, made a 76 break. On August 24, 1924 Dennis wrote to the B.A. and C.C. asking the governing body to promote an open professional snooker championship but A. Stanley Thorn, the secretary, replied: "The suggestion will receive consideration at an early date but it seems a little doubtful whether snooker as a spectacular game is sufficiently popular to warrant the successful promotion of such a competition."

George Nelson, a Leeds professional deeply involved in the promotion and trade aspects of the game, was publicly urging the B.A. and C.C. to wake up to snooker's potentialities and the indefatigable Bill Camkin produced a book of rules. The Midland Counties Billiards Association, with whom Camkin was closely associated, imposed a minimum penalty of four points for a foul stroke, contrary to the then official rules.

Camkin was also very much involved in instituting the professional snooker championship. As a proprietor of billiard halls, he knew full well how popular snooker was; and a conversation with Joe Davis, who had played snooker since his youthful days of managing billiard halls around Chesterfield, led to Davis's writing to the B.A. and C.C., drafting the conditions under which such an event could take place. The association gave their consent and issued conditions. The players were to arrange their own venues with the final at Camkin's in Birmingham; there was to be a five guinea entry fee, and a five guinea sidestake. 50 per cent of the entry fees were to be divided 6040 between winner and runner-up with the other 50 per cent for the B.A. and C.C. Gate receipts were to be divided equally between the players after expenses.

Davis, whose break of 96 with Vitalite balls against Tom Newman on February 4, 1925 had beaten Newman's professional record of 89 set in December 1919, predictably won the tournament and pocketed £6. 10s. from the gate receipts, though the Billiards Association used the players' half of the entry fees to buy a trophy. Camkin himself refereed the final in which Davis made a break of 57 and in one frame recorded runs of 32, 34 and 35 in consecutive visits. This was thought to be an exceptional sequence at the time.

The 1928 championship was played on a challenge basis with Davis exempt until the other contenders had been reduced to one. This turned out to be Fred Lawrence who, in the challenge round at Camkin's, extended Davis to 16-13. It was during this season that Davis made his first snooker century, 100, against Fred Pugh at Manchester when he took on local aspirants between sessions of a billiards match. Newman, in October 1927, had made a 97 against Davis at Thurston's, while in Sydney, Frank Smith had made a break of 116 in a 141-0 frame but this kind of feat only rated a paragraph at the time. Davis potted the first 14 reds, in a break of 95, before snookering himself on the last red against George Nelson at Otley, and Alec Mann made breaks of 99 and 106 at the Central Restaurant, Birmingham. Though chiefly preoccupied with billiards, Davis introduced snooker as a supporting attraction whenever he could—there was, after all, some mileage in being the snooker champion.

The 1929 championship attracted only five entries with Davis making a break of 61 in beating Dennis 1914 in the final and there was an increase of only one for the 1930 event in which Davis displayed his finest championship form to date, making breaks of 58, 44, 48 and 50 in the first three frames in beating Lawrence 13-2 and one of 79, a championship record, in his 25-12 win over Dennis in the final.

There was some good snooker being played in the Antipodes, notably by Murt O'Donoghue, who became the first player to clear the table from the opening stroke with a 134 in Auckland, in 1928, followed shortly afterwards with 136 and 138, and by Frank Smith with 127 at the Hotel Australia in 1931. O'Donoghue hustled throughout the 1920s in his native New Zealand and Australia prior to building up a chain of 27 billiard clubs. He became a wealthy man and never, he said, regretted his decision not to pursue the game competitively. His knowledge and skill were beyond dispute for even in his 70s, with defective eyesight, he could give striking demon strations of his skill at close quarters—especially at nursery cannons—aand was much respected as a coach.

The 1931 professional championship was a more

limited affair than ever with only two entries, and Davis defeated Dennis 25-21 in the latter's own room at Nottingham. This, though, was the toughest match Dennis ever gave the champion for he led 6-4, 14-10, 17-15 and 19-16 before Davis took the next five frames to go in front 21-19. Davis made breaks of 72, 58 and 53. In match play, the billiards players of quality seemed to have the craft to overcome those who relied more heavily on their potting. Laurie Steeples, for instance, retained in 1930 the snooker title he won in 1929 to become the second player to record the billiards and snooker double, though he was precluded from attempting a snooker hat-trick by his journey to Australia for the 1931 Empire Billiards Championship. In his absence, Matthews recorded the second of his four wins by beating Harry Kingsley 5-4 in the final.

From 1932-36, amateur snooker consolidated its popularity without its leading exponents noticeably improving their skill. There was an important rule change in 1934 when the so-called crawl stroke, rolling the cue-ball up behind a nominated free ball, was outlawed, first as a six-months experiment and then permanently.

The same period, though, saw quite spectacular advances in break-making by professionals. Horace Lindrum made an unofficial 139 break in Melbourne in March 1933; Alec Mann of Birmingham, in late-1932, took the first 12 reds, 11 blacks and a pink in a break of 95, the first time anyone in Britain had come within striking distance of the 147 maximum; Walter Lindrum made a South African record of 113 at Bulawayo in September 1933; and O'Donoghue, on September 26, 1934, playing in his own club at Griffith, New South

Wales, against Maurice O'Reilly, actually achieved the 147, not on a standard table but the first maximum nevertheless. A special certificate, signed by 135 spectators, was later presented to him.

Davis, who recorded only the centuries he made in public, still held the official record of 114 in 1933 increased the world championship record to 72 in beating Willie Smith in the final of an event which still attracted only five entries. The previous year, when he defeated McConachy, and the following year, when he defeated Newman in a match spread over three days at Nottingham and two at Kettering, saw Davis confronted by only one challenger but the championship started to widen out in 1935 when Stanbury became Canada's first entrant. As a player without any grounding in the gentler game of billiards, Stanbury constituted almost a new breed, revelling in the power shots which the billiards-snooker players tended to avoid automatically on aesthetic grounds. His own career, in retrospect, seems to have hinged on missing a simple middle pocket pink which cost him a 13-12 loss to Willie Smith, who went on, very comfortably, to reach the final. A win for Stanbury here would have established him but, as it turned out, despite many subsequent efforts and near misses, he could never quite make it.

It was this 1935 championship, however, in which Davis set a new championship record break of I 10, that established the event as a paying proposition. The following season saw the first week-long snooker matches at Thurston's where previously the game had been seen only in a supporting role to billiards or in the snooker championship itself. Horace Lindrum, aged 23, made a break of 71 at Thurston's against Newman in his first public frame in England and in 1936 became the first Australian to enter the championship. Clare O'Donnell, an even harder-hitting Canadian than Stanbury, who eccentrically kept his chalk under his bridge hand when striking, beat Sydney Lee but failed to appear for the final session when trailing Lindrurn 19-6. He did not enter again. Stanbury lost by the odd frame for the second time, 16-15 to Alec Brown, a former speedway rider, who, thus reached the semifinal at his first attempt. It seems to be unrecorded how Stanley Newman, a younger brother of Tom, came through to the semifinal but at this stage Lindrum, with a break of 101, beat him 29-2. Davis beat Brown 21-10 in the other semifinal.

The final was certainly the greatest snooker match there had yet been. Lindrum led 3-2, 6-4 and 11-9 before Davis, with breaks of 75 and 78, won four out of five on the third afternoon to lead 13-12. Lindrum levelled at 15-15; led 21-19 and 26-24 and, with the aid of a lucky snooker, won the first frame on the last day to lead 27-24. But this was as far as he got for Davis won ten in a row achieving a winning lead at 31-27 and completing the sequence at 34-27. Thurston's was packed and it was abundantly clear that snooker had become the major game, a conclusion which was underlined when the *Daily Mail* switched their Gold Cup tournament from billiards to snooker. In October 1936 *The Billiard Player* changed its name to *Billiards and Snooker.*

In December, Davis and Lindrum played the first week-long non-championship match in the provinces at Nottingham. Davis, off scratch, won the *Daily Mail*

Gold Cup tournament with five wins out of five but the great feature of the event was a new world record of 133 by Sidney Smith, the first "official" total clearance. "Thurston's Doors Locked" was one headline which eloquently stated snooker's new crowd-pulling status.

Lindrum made breaks of 141 and 135 in beating Davis 3936 in Manchester though his failure to apply for record recognition suggests the pockets may have been more generous than standard. Lindrum also beat Davis 7469 in snooker's first fortnight's match at Thurston's and regained the world break record with 135, only for Davis to equal it.

Though century breaks lower down the scale were still rare—Willie Smith's personal best, for instance, was still only 94—Davis, Lindrum, and Sidney Smith were giving clear indications of the potentialities of modern break-building snooker. Breaks were rising too on the amateur side. Kennerley held the official record with 100, though on December 3, 1935, George Hardman had made a 104 at Blackburn on a Riley standard table. Hardman, ignorant of the correct procedure, failed to apply for official recognition.

In the amateur championship, W.H. Dennis, son of Tom Dennis, made a 52 break in 1937, the year he lost to Kennerley in the final, though Kennerley himself was unquestionably the most accomplished breakmaker. He made a 10 1 break when in Australia for the Empire Billiards Championship in 1938 and created a new amateur championship record in 1939 with a break of 69, though Percy Bendon beat him 6-4 in a close 5½-hour final just as Pat Matthews had edged him out 6-5 in the 1938 final. Kennerley, who reached four consecutive amateur finals, won his second title in 1940 by beating Albert Brown, who, like him, adopted professional methods and later turned professional.

A new challenger for the professional championship emerged in the last few years before the war—Fred Davis —though his championship debut in 1937 could hardly have been less auspicious. Unknown to anyone save himself, he was starting to suffer from myopia, so it was hardly surprising that the promise he had shown in three times winning the junior professional billiards championship was not being fulfilled. Very much overshadowed by his elder brother Joe, from whom the only advice Fred received was to stop grinning while he was practising, Fred was quietly helping out in the family billiards hall in Chesterfield, unable even to tell the time accurately from the hall's large clock in order to book patrons on and off tables unless he stood directly beneath it. Selfconscious as he was, though, he told noone of his affliction, even when the balls started to look like balls of wool or even when he lost 1714 in the championship to W.A. Withers, a Welshman whom Joe immediately hammered 301. Belatedly, Fred consulted an optician and was fitted with a then revolutionary design of swivel lens spectacles. Immediately he began to play very much better, beating Herbert Holt and Alec Brown in the 1938 championship before losing honourably to Sidney Smith, then ranked only behind Joe and Lindrum.

Joe, of course, was still winning the championship with plenty to spare and in 1938 he pushed the official break record up to 138 in the Daily Mail Gold Cup.

Conceding large starts he still won the tournament with four wins out of five. The 1939 championship provided Joe with the strongest challenge he had yet encountered when Fred made a new championship record break of 113 and was beaten only 17-14 in their semifinal. In 1940 it was even closer. Fred beat Sidney Smith 17-14 in one semifinal while Joe was beating Walter Donaldson 22 9 in the other and pushed his elder brother all the way in the final before Joe clinched it 37-35 with a century break. It was to be the last time they met in the championship.

2

EQUIPMENT

The table

The standard full-size table measures approximately 12ft by 6ft. The identical nature of tables ends there. In the normal course of events you will find yourself playing on tables of excellent, mediocre and wretched quality. Some will be dead level, and others disturbingly out of true. The cloth may be new, with good nap, or it may be badly worn, shiny even. The cushions may be lively or they may be 'dead'. The pockets may be big or small not a reference to their actual size, which should be a uniform 3½ inches across, but to the amount of undercut they have. The greater the undercut, the more readily the pocket will accept the ball. This is particularly noticeable in the case of balls potted along a cushion. Temperate and humidity will affect the way any table plays.

Assuming you do not own your own table, all these factors are beyond your control. You will have to take the tables as you find them, and make what adjustments you can to the peculiarities of each. For that reason you should go out of your way to experience as wide a range of tables as possible. By doing so you will begin to find it easier and quicker to spot the good and bad points of an unfamiliar table.

As for practice, try to use a table with 'big' pockets. That will make it easier for you to pot the ball, and it is only when you are able to pot with reasonable confidence that you can concentrate on positional play. If you learn to play on tight tables you will need to concern yourself so much simply with potting the next ball that you will be unable to develop the rhythm and fluency necessary for break-building.

Smaller tables for the home are becoming increasingly popular, and their quality much improved. They are fun to play on, adequate for practising basic technique and ideal for introducing youngsters to the game. Steve Davis learned to play on a quarter-size table, which is as good a recommendation as any. Beyond a certain age, and a certain standard of skill, however, the real challenge of snooker can only be met by playing on a full-size table.

The balls

As with the tables, you will have to take the balls as you find them which is generally very good these days. The original heavy ivory balls are a thing of the distant past. They were superseded before the Second World War by lighter Crystalate balls. In recent years Crystalate balls have given way to Super Crystalate, which are entirely synthetic and ideally suited to the demands of the game. They are more lively than the Crystalate balls, which means they take spin more readily, thereby maximizing your opportunities for cue ball control the key to snooker.

The cue

You are strongly advised to buy your own cue. No two cues play alike, so it is foolish to handicap yourself each time you play by having to come to terms with an unfamiliar one. It can be likened to playing the violin. Even a rank beginner would know better than to practise with bows picked at random.

The top professionals, with a single exception, guard their cues with their lives. The exception is the brilliant young Canadian, Kirk Stevens. He is not at all obsessional about his cue, regarding it as a bit of timber essential to his trade. The others shake their heads in disbelief at this eccentricity. For them, losing or damaging their cue is a horrific prospect. Once they have settled on a cue, early in their careers, they look forward hopefully to a lifelong partnership. Terry Griffiths reckons his to be about eighty years old. It is by conventional standards too thin and much too light, but that means nothing to him. It feels right, and therefore it is right for him. John Spencer won his first two World Championships with a battered old cue that was warped. He claimed to feel lost with any other.

Starting from scratch, you will naturally choose a straight cue. The recommended weight is about 17 ounces, and it should taper down to a tip of about 10mm diameter. The butt should fit comfortably in the hand, and the cue should feel balanced reassuringly heavy in the shaft. The normal length is about 4ft 10in. The best cues are made of either ash maple. Ash has a more visible grain and Steve Davis for one prefers that because it enables him to hold the cue in the same position for each shot. Others prefer the more subdued grain of maple. Make sure there is a ferrule fitted to the tip end. This metal plastic ring protects the end again splitting, and also against accident damage when fitting and filing new tip.

There are advantages to a two-piece cue. It is much more convenient to carry around, and it is less prone warping. For the really serious player it has another advantage as well. By buying two identical tip section and breaking both in, you have an immediate solution to any crisis caused by the tip coming off, or wearing down too much, during play. The reason most of the professionals use a one-piece cue is that they settled on their cue before the two-piece type was perfected. In the dreaded event of having to search out a new cue, most think they would turn to a two-piece.

Cue care

Because of its importance to your game, your cue needs the best of care. Do not lean it up against a wall, which encourages warping. Lay it flat if you are not using it for a few minutes. When you are not playing, always return it to its case. When storing the cue, avoid extremes of hot and cold. Keep the cue clean with a damp cloth, and make sure your hands are clean before you play.

The leather tip is the only point of contact with the cue ball, and players are therefore extremely fussy about its condition. The tip should be firm yet resilient, to allow a certain amount of grip on the ball. You will soon develop a feel for the tip you will know when it is right, and when it needs attention.

It is a good idea to learn to replace a worn tip yourself, a simple enough task and a satisfying one. File the bottom of the new tip and the end of the cue flat and clean. Then stick the tip on with either quick-drying or contact adhesive. When it is secure, file it into the classic domelike shape, being careful always to file downwards so as not to risk dislodging the tip,

When the tip becomes shiny through use it will fail to hold chalk. Tapping it gently with a file will roughen it up.

The rests

Such is the size of a snooker table that it is frequently impossible for even the tallest player to reach the cue ball—and it is important to reach the cue ball without overstretching. Several implements are designed to overcome this problem.

First there is the ordinary rest, which is sufficient to get you within comfortable reach of the cue ball most of the time. Sometimes it will not be long enough, in which case you must turn to the half butt, which is a long cue with long rest. And there are occasions when even the half butt is too short for your needs. The three-quarter butt is a nine-foot version of the half butt, a monstrous thing that no one would willingly use. Just as unpopular is the spider, a rest with a raised head which enables you to bridge at a distance over an intervening ball or balls near the cue ball. The cue extension is a recent and useful invention, and there are various types of manufacture. They fit snugly over the butt of the cue, and this allows a player to retain some of the feel of playing with his own cue—and of course tip—on certain shots that would otherwise require the use of the cumbersome and frequently ill-tipped half butt.

2

PLAYING TO WIN

Break-building

Snooker is a game of immeasurable variety the subject of break-building is inexhaustible. No player has ever got to the end of it and none ever will. If you were to suggest to Steve Davis that it must all be pretty old hat to him by now he would realize you knew nothing about snooker. He will remain fascinated by break-building for the rest of his playing life. It is the core of his game, and in his quest for snooker perfection he will ponder it, practise it and dismay his opponents with deadly demonstrations of it for as long as he remains on top of the world of snooker. His safety play is of course exemplary, but it is his superior break-building, over the long haul of a long season, that first put him and still keeps him at the front of the pack.

You should consider it reassuring that the most exhilarating aspect of snooker is also the most important. At whatever level you play, that will always be the case. The rank novice who pays attention to his cue action and studies the angles will quickly gain a measure of confidence in potting. He will quickly get into the habit of thinking in positional terms, which means he will stand an excellent chance of following a red with a colour. For the novice, that two-ball sequence is in itself a useful break, and he may well extend it with another red and colour. He will beat the spots off a fellow novice who contents himself with potting the easiest red in the hope that a colour will then miraculously present itself. The club player who really applies himself to the challenge of scoring twenty four points when he is amongst three loose reds around the black spot will always pull away from an opponent who is pleased to take a red and a black and then run for safety. And so it goes, right to the top of the game.

Control around the black

Nothing could be more apparent from watching televised snooker than the supreme importance of control around the black. The really enormous breaks feature it almost exclusively, even if in the course of some total or near total clearances the player is forced to take the odd lower-value colour in order to sustain the break. Useful, and even frame-winning breaks can be and are fashioned around the pink, but such breaks appear to be constructed rather painfully. Certainly break-building on the pink never rattles along with the apparent ease that you are accustomed to seeing when the action is around the black.

An obvious reason why players favour the black is that it is the highest scoring ball on the table. But that is not the principal reason. By design or happy accident, the game was devised in such a way that the most valuable colour happens to be far and away the best positioned for break-building. As play normally unfolds, no other colour is so well placed for establishing and continuing the red-colour, sequence. The pink on its spot will go into any pocket, but it is much further from the top pockets than the black is. More to the point, it is much further from the top cushion. It is the fact that the black spot is close to the reds, close to the top pockets and close to the top cushion that sets it apart as the premier ball for break-building. Endless use of the top cushion is made in the black ball game. It is quite inconceivable to imagine a really big break made without it. It is fair to say that if the rules of snooker were changed by swopping black and blue spots, say, players would stay at the top of the table and content themselves with the lower-value colour. As for the baulk colours, they play no part in serious break-building except as a fall-back position for keeping a break going when it would otherwise be stymied.

The red-black sequence

You will encounter endless permutations of break-building opportunities around the black spot, and practice will help you to gain assurance when presented with them. There are two golden rules to keep in mind. First, be careful about leaving yourself straight on the black. If you do, you restrict your positional range to the line of the shot doubly disadvantageous because it rules out possible use of the top cushion. There are occasions when a six-inch screw back or six-inch run-through are all you need, but often dead straight will get you into positional trouble where a wide range of other angles will not. Second, clear the path between the black spot and both top pockets at the earliest opportunity. That way you maximize your scope for potting the black, which is particularly important if you come a little adrift in positional terms after potting a red.

To practise, you can simply scatter a few reds in the vicinity of the black and take it from there. If you group four reds as indicated, all the principal features of blackball play will present themselves.

1. Taking Red 2 straight into the top left pocket is an arbitrary choice. Screw back to leave a three-quarter ball angle on the black.
2. Pot the black plain ball and bounce off the cushion to leave a choice of all the other reds. If instead of doing that you were to stun off the top cushion, thereby coming back the other side of the reds, you would be committing yourself to Red 3. In general, do not attempt to gain pinpoint position on one red when you can have adequate position on several.
3. You are just off straight on Red 1, which is ideal because by getting rid of Red 1 both remaining reds become pottable in either pocket. A little screw shot should leave you with that familiar three-quarter ball angle on the black.
4. In fact, you have come slightly too straight on the black. Pot the black with top and right-hand side, to bring the cue ball off top and side cushions into position for both remaining reds. When using side, it is especially important to follow through smoothly because you are not striking the cue ball at its point of maximum density.
5. You are straight on Red 4, so simply run through for the black, aiming again for the three-quarter ball angle.
6. Screw off the black for the final red.

7. Pot the red plain ball and bounce off the cushion to leave yourself comfortably on the black.
8. Pot black.

Sustaining a break by using the blue

You will often find yourself in a position where the only pottable red must result i your sending the cue ball down the table away from the black and pink. Sometimes you will have to go all the way down to the baulk colours; other times you will be able to pull up for the blue. In this example, you are too thin on the red to hold the cue ball for the pink. Even pocket weight on the red would only succeed in putting the cue ball somewhere near the blue but the wrong side of it and as thin as quarter-ball on the pink. You should accept that you are at least for the moment out of business on the pink.

1 Go positively for a positional shot on the blue, rather than just hope it emerges. Pot the red with screw and a touch of left-hand side. Ideally you want to be three-quarter ball on the blue (A), but half-ball will do (B).

2 If A, simply stun the blue and you will come nicely on to the last red, with black to follow.

3 B is more difficult, but certainly achievable. Stun the cue ball off the top cushion with a touch of left-hand side. In either case, once you are firmly on that final red the table is at your mercy.

Sometimes a player slightly over-hits and comes past both A and B, but then is able to rescue himself by potting the blue straight to the corner pocket. Take this as a favourable run of the balls and do not rely on it.

Sustaining a break by using the baulk colours

When you run out of position on the black and pink, the blue is not always available to rescue you. It may be near a cushion, or some reds may be blocking its path to a suitable pocket. Alternatively, the blue itself may be in the open but you have left yourself on a red in such a way that in potting it you will not be able to hold the cue ball for the blue into a middle pocket. You are therefore forced to look to the baulk colours to sustain your break. In such circumstances, go positively for position on one or more of the baulk colours, rather than simply float the cue ball towards baulk in the hope that something suitable will materialize.

1 In this example, you cannot hold for the blue because the potting angle on the red is too thin. Take the cue ball off both side cushions for a baulk colour. Any one of the three will do, which gives you a good margin. The only rule is never to go beyond the baulk line when trying to sustain a break using a baulk colour. From behind the baulk line you could easily lay a snooker on the remaining red, but that is distinctly inferior to keeping the break going in this case right through to a clearance, which is decidedly on.

2 You are on all three colours, but the three-quarter ball green is ideal for screwing back up for the final red.

3 In this example you are straight on the brown, with the yellow and green well away from their spots. A simple screw shot would take you along path A, but if you play the shot with screw and left-hand side the cue ball will follow path B. In either case

you should pot the last red, but by taking the'B'option you will be able to make the red so much easier that you can devote more of your concentration to leaving the most advantageous angle on the black to gain position on the yellow.

Clearing the colours

Even in the most closely fought matches, the top professionals routinely defeat each other by thumping margins in individual frames. That is because they are all capable of taking decisive advantage of positional openings when they occur. Frequently a good opening appears very early in the frame—even from the break-off -which means that the frame may be effectively decided then and there. You will often have seen one player sitting quietly in his chair while his opponent runs up an opening break of eighty or more. From that point he is just a spectator like everyone else, curious to see how far the break will be extended. He has lost the frame, painlessly enough in this case since once that big break began to unfold the outcome was beyond his control. There is every chance that he will turn the tables next frame, and get away with as big a break or bigger.

When it's all on the colours

At less exalted levels of play, frame scores, as opposed to match scores, tend to be nothing like so lopsided. Where a good break is considered to be twenty, there is ample opportunity to keep alive in a frame. For players of roughly equal ability, it is the rule rather than the exception for them to arrive at the colours with everything still to play for. That being so, nothing could be more useful than knowing how to go about clearing the colours in a single trip to the table. This is not as easy as it is so often made to look on television, but if you understand the basic principles involved you will at least be able to make a realistic attempt. How you fare thereafter will depend upon your ability to execute positional strokes as you intend them.

Obviously the six colours can be left anywhere on the table, some or even all of them in unpottable positions, the cue ball miles from the yellow or whatever. However, the better the standard of play, the more likely they are to be sitting on their spots. For practice, assume that they are, that you have potted the final red, followed it with a colour and deliberately come into ideal position on the yellow. It is very important that you get into the habit of approaching the final red-colour sequence with yellow in mind.

Make the pots easy

Note how comparatively simple all the pots are, given accurate positional strokes. Consider how easily the sequence can break down with one bad positional shot. You may rescue yourself temporarily with a good pot, but the chances are you will have to follow it with an even better pot. How long will you be able to sustain a break that makes such heavy demands on your potting ability?

You may be interested to know that Steve Davis attempts this routine literally endlessly. That is, he clears from yellow to black, and in potting the black brings the cue ball back down the table for position on the yellow. Then he re-spots the balls and starts all over again. And so on, and on ...

1 You have a three-quarter ball angle possibly slightly fuller on the yellow. Screw back for the

green. Should you be somewhere between three-quarter and half-ball on the yellow you would have to stun the cue ball off the side cushion to come on to the same position for the green.

2 Three-quarter ball on the green is ideal, although anything between that and straight will do nicely. Less than Three-quarter and you will need to come off the side cushion for the brown. If you go more than a fraction past straight you will leave yourself the more difficult task of potting the green and bouncing off the bottom cushion for position on the brown. Pot the green and screw back for the brown, aiming to leave yourself between half-ball and three-quarter ball on it.

3 You are nearly half-ball on the brown, which is fine. This is the most testing positional shot of the sequence because of the distance the cue ball must travel. Pot the brown and stun off the side cushion to come three-quarter ball on the blue. If you come much less than three-quarter ball you will have difficulty in holding the cue ball for the pink. Straight on the blue will leave you with an eminently missable pink. But the worst thing you can do is to get above the blue. You would then be sending the cue ball away from the pink as you potted the blue. You see the professionals negotiate this difficulty with ease, bringing the cue ball around off three cushions for the pink, but not only do they have the cue power for the job, they have a fine, fast-moving championship cloth to help them.

4 Pot the three-quarter ball blue and run through for a three-quarter ball pink. Again, the real pitfall here is to run past straight on the pink. There is no

problem if you can still pot the pink three-quarter ball and come off the side cushion, but if you leave a half-ball pot you will have an unfavourable angle to get on the black.

5 Pot the three-quarter ball pink and stun for black.

6 A simple three-quarter ball black.

Clearing the colours from the 'D'

There can be any number of variations in the early stages of clearing all the colours from their spots, depending upon the position on the yellow. The positional shot from black to yellow is obviously one of the most critical in the game. Your intention will be to gain ideal position, but you will not always succeed. Sometimes this will be because you simply play a poor or mediocre shot in potting the black. Other times, you will have left yourself on the black in such a way that in potting it you have no realistic chance of getting down the table for yellow, With a reasonable angle a long or longish pot on the yellow is quite feasible, although at a critical stage in a frame it carries considerable risk. Finally, you may find yourself with less than ideal position on the yellow through no fault of your own. Your opponent has gone in-off, leaving the colours on their spots. You are therefore starting the clearance with the cue ball in the 'U. Because this particular circumstance crops up now and again in real play, clearing the colours from the'D' is worth practising.

1 Place the cue ball so as to give yourself a three-quarter ball angle on the yellow into the middle pocket. Straight may be the easier pot, but it will not leave you as well placed on the green. In

attempting such pots into the middle aim for the far jaw of the pocket, from where it will drop if more than half the ball is over the edge. If you touch the near jaw it will almost always throw it out.

2a The pot on the yellow, assuming you make it, should leave you more or less half-ball on the green three quarter ball if you can get the cue ball to travel further. The pot is not difficult, but you have a bewildering array of positional opportunities on the brown. You can play the green slowly and bring the cue ball off the side cushion to achieve conventional position on the brown. The difficulty with attempting this shot is that you must play it slowly, and slow shots, especially against or across the nap, have a habit of drifting off line. On a poor table you can almost guarantee it.

2b To avoid that hazard you can play the shot with greater strength, attempting to bring the cue ball back to the other side of the brown, so that the brown can be potted in the same baulk pocket as the green.

2c Or you can play it stronger still, to come off both side cushions and leave the cue ball a little further up table but still on the brown.

2d Either 2b or 2c is feasible, but this is better. If you stun the green with medium pace you should obtain good position off one cushion. Note that you need to be able to play all these shots, not necessarily in clearing the colours, but because all of them may be demanded at some stage of the frame.

From there, you continue the clearance as previously described. Whatever the position from which you begin to clear the spotted colours, you must aim to sort yourself out by the time you get to the brown, because the positional shot from brown to blue is a critical one. Yellow, green and brown are in close proximity, but for blue you are moving into a different area of the table. It is admittedly possible to make a pot on the blue from virtually anywhere on the table and achieve position on the pink, but you would not want to gamble a frame on it. Even for the professionals, brown for blue is likely to be the key shot in the colour clearance.

Clearing the colours

This is a very advanced exercise, indeed a testing one even for the professionals. It provides a harsh examination of anyone's cue ball control.

1 Pot the yellow three-quarter ball into the middle pocket, running through to come almost straight on the green.

2 Screw from the green to three-quarter ball on the brown.

3 Screw sharply from the brown to leave a three-quarter ball or slightly fuller angle on the blue. There is not much margin of error here, and accuracy is difficult, to say the least.

4 A plain ball shot on the b pocket weight, coming three-quarter ball on to the pink.

5 Stun the pink, to come as straight as possible on to the black.

6 Stun the black.

If you can do all that, you may with some justification consider that you can afford to give this book to a less accomplished friend.

The line-up

This is a first-rate practice routine, much favoured by professionals. You do not have to be of their standard to profit from it, but you must have progressed to a point where positional play is within your grasp. You must, in other words, have an adequate command of screw and stun strokes, and that implies a reasonable understanding of where the cue ball is likely to wind Lip after you have played them.

The fifteen reds are arranged as shown in diagram 1, with all the colours on their spots. For the opening shot you can place the cue ball where you wish. Pot a red, then any colour, then another red, another colour and so on. See how far you get without breaking down. Note your score and keep trying to improve on it. When you get to the stage at which you can clear the fifteen reds you will be a good player indeed. Along the way, you will learn a vast amount about positional play, and what you learn will be directly applicable to countless break-building opportunities in the future.

The sequence can be played in an infinite number of ways, and as long as you can keep potting the balls, one is as good as another. The example analysed here is as it was actually played by Clive Everton. It will pay you to study it closely, and more than once. In terms of break-building, and the sort of thinking as well as stroke-play that has to go into it, it is a complete lesson.

1 Choose what red you want, but Red 1 is as good as any. Straight pot into the top pocket, screwing back for position on the black. The screw must be carefully controlled, as always. Uncontrolled screw is worse than useless. Not far enough and you will be right on top of the black with a quarter-ball angle on it. That pot can be difficult, and the cue ball awkward to control. Screw back too far and you will come almost straight on the black. You will have increased the distance between cue ball and object ball, thereby making the next pot more difficult really difficult if you have come close enough to the cushion to necessitate awkward bridging. And you will have too thick an angle on the black to gain position easily on another red. The ideal is about three-quarter ball, as here.

2 Pot the black and stun off the top cushion, aiming to come back into position for Red 2 and Red 3. The worst pitfall here is to leave yourself short above Red 2. It would not matter if you played a little over strength, coming on to Red 4. Further than that brings you towards the side cushion. Too much screw will widen the angle at which the cue ball comes on to the top cushion, in which case it will end up close to the side cushion. There is a general point here. Always try to leave yourself far enough off the cushions so that you can make your bridge reasonably comfortably on the bed of the table.

3 You have many choices for the next red, but consider Red 2 and Red 3. For Red 2 the potting angle is just too thin to allow you to hold position on the black with a soft screw shot. You would

have to stun off the top cushion to get on to the black. That would not be particularly difficult, but it is not advisable to bring a cushion into play when you have an equally good shot that does not require it. When you use a cushion, you have two factors to take into account: the speed of the table and the speed of the cushions. It is easier to deal with the speed of the table alone. Red 3 is just as good a shot, so it is the better choice. It is three-quarter ball or a little fuller, so run through, aiming to leave yourself with something like a half-ball angle on the black. At this stage, Red 3 is better than Red 2 for strategic reasons as well. It opens a gap between remaining reds. As the break continues, such gaps become important because they increase the positional margins of error.

4 Pot the black plain ball at slow-medium pace. Pace is everything with plain ball shots, because it is your only control. The object here is for the cue ball to come off the top cushion into position on Red 2. That means you want to be roughly level with Red 4 and Red 5, to leave yourself a three-quarter ball angle on Red 2. Falling badly short would be serious. Coming too far would not be as serious because there is always Red 4, and several possibilities for the middle pocket.

5 This three-quarter ball angle on Red 2 is perfect. It allows you to screw gently back for the black. The important thing here is not to finish dead straight on the black. If you do, you will then have to screw straight back off the side cushion for the following shot. By no means impossible, but the trick always is to make minimal demands on your technique.

Worse than dead straight on the black would be to wind up above it. Try *never* to leave yourself above the black. Cutback shots are always more difficult because the pocket is out of vision. In this particular case, depending upon the angle, a cutback shot would send the cue ball somewhere into the reds. If you start to scatter the reds around, anything could happen.

6 Three-quarter ball on the black is fine. Play it plain ball, aiming to bring the cue ball a foot or so off the side cushion. This will leave you several choices. You could, if you chose, screw the cue ball directly up beside the reds, thereby avoiding the use of the cushion, but it would be slightly more difficult, with no prospect of positional benefit.

7 Now is the time to turn your back on the red-black sequence, and open up some space between the blue and pink spots. Otherwise, you will find your options narrowing later on. Being almost straight on Red 8 is a happy accident, because you can pot it without disturbing a red either side. But while Red 8 may be the clear choice of pot, there are two alternative ways to play the shot. You can screw back for the pink into the top right-hand pocket, or run through for the pink into the top left-hand pocket. Your choice should be governed by the fact that you will want to be between three-quarter ball and straight on the pink, both for potting ease and so as not to cannon into other reds.

Once you realize that, your choice is made for you. If you screw back, you must be accurate with your screw to about 2½ balls' width, to get the desired angle. If you run through, you have almost double that margin. If to gain that safety margin you had to accept a more difficult pot on the pink, you would have to weigh the respective advantages and disadvantages very carefully, but in this case there is not much in it. Run through Red 8.

8 Pot the pink with gentle screw, aiming to be more or less straight on Red 4. This is a fairly easy positional shot, but it is the longest pot to date.

9 A change of plans here. There is nothing whatever wrong with Red 4. Just a matter of potting it and running through for the black into the right-hand pocket. But look at Red 7. It is just as easy to pot it into the middle. Given the way things stand now, Red 7 might prove slightly more awkward at a later stage. The lesson here is that even when you get perfectly into position as intended, always survey the table to see if you have actually left yourself an even better shot. Do not try to adhere rigidly to any plan in break-building. Be flexible, always responding to the pattern of the balls. Red 7 is three-quarter ball or a little fuller. A gentle screw shot should bring you straight on the pink. Be careful not to leave yourself short. Even an inch short of straight on the pink would necessitate the use of the rest. It is better to risk going a little too far rather than have that happen.

10 Perfect on the pink, leaving a choice of run-through or screw for the next position. Run-through is dangerous because you would need to be inch perfect. There is never much of a margin when you get in so close amongst the balls. You want a bit of elbow room, so screw back off the pink. That is bound to leave you with ample choice. However,

guard against excessive use of screw, which would bring you uncomfortably near the side cushion.

11 Note that the cue ball has not screwed back dead on line. The nap of the cloth has caused it to fall away slightly, a matter of no consequence in this instance but a factor you should be aware of. Sometimes it is of consequence. Choices now abound, but Red 10 is best. It is just off straight into the middle pocket, but not sufficiently so to cause the cue ball to cannon into a neighbouring red. Here again, you can either run through or screw back. Run through would leave a longer and therefore more difficult pink. Screw is the better choice.

12 A three-quarter ball angle on the pink is fine. A gentle screw will leave you on three reds. Ideally, Red 5 would be best because it would open a gap.

13 Red 5 it is, although there is no way of holding the cue ball for ideal position on pink into the middle. Therefore you must be looking for the black. You could run through gently for it, but there are distinct advantages to playing more boldly. Play the shot with sufficient strength to bring the cue ball off the side cushion, up towards the black. It makes for a much easier black.

14 The second advantage to playing Red 5 that way can now be seen. The cue ball is so positioned that the top cushion will not have to be used in this shot and it is the most demanding shot yet. The three-quarter ball angle on the black will bring the cue ball down the table, which is what you want. You could play it plain ball, but if you did you would

need perfect strength to bring the cue ball off the side cushion and nicely on to a red. That is always the difficulty with plain ball, the need for perfect strength. There are plenty of places along that plain ball path where you would find yourself in a real mess. Screw is the answer, but here again you have to get it right. If you screw too much, you might cannon into Red 4. If you screw too little you will finish up close to the side cushion.

15 The three-quarter ball angle on Red 4 is fine. Now, however, it is time to take stock. The low and middle-numbered reds have been disappearing nicely, and there are plenty of useful gaps between those remaining. It is about time to open up some space around the blue spot. If you leave all those high-numbered reds to the end, one bad positional shot could easily end the break, because you would have nowhere else on the table to look for a loose red that might let you rescue the situation. For as long as possible, you want to keep your options open. Now is the time to prepare for some work around the blue spot. You must pot Red 4 and get on to the black. This time, however, you want to leave yourself nearer half-ball than three-quarter ball on the black. That way you will not need such weight of shot to bring the cue ball off the top cushion and down to the middle of the table. But you do not want to be too thin on the black because that would endanger the pot. A gentle screw shot on Red 4 should do the job.

16 The near half-ball angle on the black is what you wanted. It is best to play it plain ball, because if you apply too much screw you could end up close

to the side cushion. Plain ball with a hint of top is perfectly safe. There are no reds in the way and the cue ball is certain to miss the pink and end up decently positioned somewhere in the centre of the table.

17 Both Red 11 and Red 12 are on, but Red 12 is better for two reasons. It opens a gap and from it you should be able to screw back to get almost straight on the blue.

18 The blue is almost straight. Screw back for choice of Red 14 and Red 15.

19 You are now perfectly positioned to clear up all the reds around the blue spot, before going back up the table to finish the job. Pot Red 14 and run through for a nearly straight blue.

20 Pot the blue and run through to leave yourself on Red 15.

21 Pot Red 15 and run through to leave an almost straight blue. It is vital to keep to the baulk side of blue.

22 Roll in the blue, which leaves you just off straight on Red 13.

23 The important thing about Red 13 is that you must, following the pot, leave the cue ball to the baulk side of the blue, so that when you pot the blue you will come on to Red 11. You can either run through Red 13 to be one side of the blue, or screw back to be the other. There is nothing in it.

24 Having screwed back slightly baulk side of the blue, screw the blue into the side pocket, hoping to

get on Red 11. If you fail to get nicely on Red 11, you will have Red 6 into the right-hand corner.

25 Red11 and Red6 are both on, and both at the favourable three-quarter ball angle. On reflection, there is nothing whatever to choose between them, so for variety's sake it is reasonable to switch to Red 6. Play a stun shot on Red 6, taking care to leave the cue ball slightly up table from straight on the pink. That is, ensure that you have something like a three-quarter ball angle to your right. If you leave a three-quarter angle to your left, you will in the course of potting the pink take the cue ball away from the remaining reds.

26 Pot the pink with gentle screw, with the intention of leaving yourself with either a three-quarter ball angle on Red 9 into the top corner or a three-quarter ball angle on Red 11 into the middle.

27 The angle on Red 11 is fine, but it is critical that the cue ball should end up on the baulk side of the blue. Otherwise, in potting the blue you will send the cue ball away from Red 9. It would be a pity to break down now I Run through Red 11.

28 Pot the blue and run through with right-hand side off the side cushion for Red 9. Note that this is the first and only use of side in the course of a thirty-shot sequence. Not quite typical, perhaps, but it indicates how close-range work depends so heavily on simple little screw, stun and run-through shots to the exclusion of side. You must always have a good reason for using side. In this case, running side brings you closer to the final red.

29 This position is pretty well ideal for clearing the table. Being almost straight on Red 9, you are able to run through for the blue. The blue leads you naturally on to the yellow. Red 9 should be played plain ball with a hint of top, and the weight is critical. You want the cue ball slightly up table from the blue. Not too much up table, because that would make it difficult to pot the blue and hold the cue ball for the yellow. Not straight on the blue, because that would make it impossible for you to get any closer to the yellow than the line running between the middle pockets, Worst of all would be to get baulk side of the blue. That would take the cue ball away from the yellow.

30 Pot the blue, using soft screw to come straight on to the yellow.

Having come this far, you should have little difficulty in mopping up the colours!

Looking ahead

When on television you watch a really big break a century clearance, say, or on very rare occasions even a 147 you might be tempted to think that the player has planned the break at least in outline before potting the first red. He has not. It would be beyond human capacity to plot that far ahead, and in any case it would be meaningless to make the attempt because it is impossible to pot with such positional accuracy as to follow any scenario for thirty shots or more. What a good player does do, however, is assess the lie of the table, and relate it to the stage of the game. He can see that the reds are nicely positioned for a productive spell around the black spot, or that in the course of snapping up two loose reds he must open the pack in order to continue the break, or that a particular ball must be developed from an unpottable position, and so forth. More immediately, he must always took at least two shots ahead. That is, before he pots one red, he not only must have clear positional intention for the colour to follow, but similar designs on the next red. That is the only way of fashioning a substantial break. Forward planning, therefore, really comes down to selecting the shot that best furthers your aim of monopolizing the table and therefore the scoreboard.

1 This three-quarter ball angle on the black is ideal for disturbing the pack. And now is the time to do it, because you have an easy red as insurance should the pack not open in a favourable way.

2 Being a little more than half-ball on the black, it is relatively easy to stun into the unpottable reds, which should with any luck run into such position that a total clearance is at least a possibility.

3 Screw off the halt to three-quarter ball black so as to dislodge the last remaining red from the side cushion.

4 You have potted a red but failed to gain good position on a colour. Suppose you are forty points ahead. All you need worry about is letting your opponent in with a winning clearance, You want, therefore, to play a safety stroke on the pink in such a way as to leave the pink tight on the side cushion.

5 This is an identical situation to 4, except that in this case you are forty points behind. Now it is you who needs the total clearance, and therefore you will want to play a safety stroke on the pink in

such a way as to leave it in the open. That way, if your safety stroke forces an error from your opponent the table is at least theoretically at your mercy.

The break of the championship

The essence of successful break-building is to play each shot in such a way as to make the following one as easy as possible. The more difficult any particular pot is, the greater the likelihood that the break will come to an abrupt end. That is self-evident theory, and as you gain skill at positional play you will automatically apply it to the best of your ability. Your success at snooker depends upon it.

In reality, however, things often work out quite differently. Either you are faced with a difficult shot from which the positional outcome is dubious, or you make a positional error. It happens all the time, at any level, and when it does you either have to adopt safety tactics or accept the challenge of a difficult pot. The particular circumstances of the frame will affect the choice, but you will often have seen the professionals take on a difficult pot and make it only to leave themselves facing another, and take that on successfully, only to leave themselves with yet another difficult pot, and so on. To fashion a break in this manner puts enormous strains on anyone's potting ability, particularly under matchplay conditions. The following sequence has entered snooker history as being quite remarkable.

In the 1982 Embassy World Championship semifinal, Alex Higgins stood on the brink of defeat. He had played very well but Jimmy White had played brilliantly to lead him 1513. From this position, two down with three to play, Higgins retrieved one frame with a break of 72, but White led 59-0 in the next. White therefore needed only to pot three more balls to leave Higgins needing a snooker. He had been potting everything, but after an opening break of 41 he had missed a routine black, and now at 59 he missed a red using the rest. Had he potted that red, his excellent position on the pink would virtually have guaranteed him a place in the final. Even as it was, the odds were that he would still get at least one more chance to clinch frame and match, because there was an unpottable red just baulk side of the middle pocket.

Higgins has an enviable habit of playing well when his back is to the wall, but this really was a desperate plight, to put it mildly.

1 Initially, the only pottable red was one to the right-hand corner. In potting it, Higgins completely misjudged the strength of his shot and left himself short on the pink when virtually any position on the left-hand side of the table along the line the cue ball was travelling would have left an easy pink. The blue was not only a very difficult pot, with the intended pocket out of vision, but it offered no subsequent position without an exceptional shot.

2 Higgins could have played a safety shot as there were just enough reds left to win without the aid of snookers, but deciding that the time had come for do or die measures he swept in the long green knowing that if he missed it he had almost certainly played his last shot. By a curious irony, having been forced into this deep trouble by missing position on the pink, he had, in fact, the angle on the green that allowed him to develop the awkward red into a pottable position.

3 Meanwhile, the only pottable red was a thin cut to the left an corner pocket, which made it difficult to control the speed of the cue ball. If the cue ball had rebounded out of baulk he would have had a choice of black into the middle pocket or one of the baulk colours. Instead, it finished within the 'D' without leaving the angle he wanted on any of the baulk colours in order to get the cue ball up the table for the next red.

4 Higgins could have played a snooker by rolling tight to the yellow, but as he said afterwards, 'I was in no mood for snookers.' He selected black again, knowing that he was finished if he missed it because the cue ball would automatically roll into a position from which at least one, possibly two reds would be eminently pottable.

5 Concentrating fiercely to pot the black, he did not run the cue ball quite far enough for what would have been his preferred red, the one slightly left-most in the diagram, although he knew of course that the red nearest the middle pocket would be pottable virtually wherever the cue ball finished past the blue spot. This red, however, did require quite a delicate snick, and not too much pace could be used. When potting at an acute angle into the middle pocket the ball can only enter it off its jaws, and excessive pace will therefore cause the ball to jump out.

6 Being somewhat restricted in his positional options, Higgins played to leave himself on the blue, but not at the angle at which he finished. Undaunted, he produced the shot of the break, potting the blue with screw and extreme left-hand side. The latter

caused the cue ball to spin very sharply off the side cushion, and travel back up the table towards the reds. He actually hit this shot too well'. His intention was to leave the left-most red to the right corner pocket, but the cue ball travelled too far.

7 Another difficult pot, piling on the pressure. He made a beautiful long red to the baulk pocket and screwed across for the black, prime position at last.

8 Now a straightforward black from its spot, screwing out for one of the loose reds.

9 He potted the penultimate red with the rest, bouncing the cue ball off the cushion for the black.

10 A half or three-quarter ball angle on the black would have made it easier to get position on the last red, but from straight on the black he screwed back off the side cushion to leave the last red to the middle.

11 He stunned the last red into the middle pocket, taking care to leave the kind of angle on the black that makes it easy to get on the yellow.

12 By now Higgins had done all the hard work, and that in itself imposes a special kind of pressure because the player now knows that he cannot be defeated by the difficulty of the situation, only by his own frailty. Mercurial though he may be, Higgins tends to be very reliable in these circumstances. From the black, he played the cue ball off the top cushion with a touch of left-hand side into perfect position on the yellow, with the colours on their spots.

13 The yellow was just a shade off straight, but it was an easy matter to screw for green.

14 From point-blank range he potted the green, screwing gently for brown.

15 From the three-quarter ball brown" Higgins screwed directly back f the blue.

16 The pink was a bit below its spot and the table running very fast, so it would have been dangerous simply to roll the blue in because the cue ball could have finished awkwardly on the pink. Instead, he screwed sharply back to leave himself a straight pink.

17 He potted the pink with ease.

18 A simple black for the frame.

Summarizing for the BBC, John Spencer described this clearance as 'the break of the Championship'. No one argued. It brought Higgins level at 1515. He then won the final frame and went on to defeat Ray Reardon 1815 in the final.

Safety play

Safety play becomes an increasingly important aspect of the game as your standard of play 'improves. At the pinnacle of the game it is as significant as potting, and you will frequently have been absorbed by the nail-biting spectacle of two great players engaged in a desperate battle of wits as they try to deny each other a potting opportunity. At the other end of the scale, the complete novice has little incentive to consider safety play, except when he is presented with an obvious opportunity. His opponent, assuming he is of roughly equivalent standard ' will not be so dangerous as to justify making his life unduly difficult. He is not going to amass a winning break just because you have let him in Conversely, if by playing a safety stroke a novice subsequently gets a favourable position himself, he is unlikely to be able to capitalize on it in the way that a more experienced player can. The novice is therefore advised to concentrate on potting and break-building, leaving the subtleties of safety tactics to a later stage, when the need for them will be readily apparent. It is disheartening to see novices engaging in grim safety battles when they should be developing potting skills.

There are a few situations that obviously dictate a safety stroke, where there is nothing pottable, for instance, or when you need snookers to win. Beyond that, there are no hard and fast rules. The lie of the balls, the state of the game, or the match, the player's feeling of confidence, or lack of it all these factors must influence the decision whether to attempt a pot or play for safety. It is a question of weighing the odds. What are your chances of making the pot, the way you are feeling at that moment, and, if you do make it, is it likely to bring significant profit? If you miss it, what are you likely to leave your opponent? If you opt for safety, can you leave your opponent in real difficulty, preferably snookered?

Aggressive safety shots

Leaving your opponent in deep trouble should be the goal of all safety Play. It is not good enough to adopt a purely negative approach spoiling tactics designed just to keep your opponent from scoring. Snooker is a game of initiative, and safety play should be viewed as a means of keeping or seizing the initiative. A positive safety shot is one that attempts to stretch your opponent to breaking point. It is one that tries to leave him with such a difficult shot that he is likely in his turn to leave you with a scoring opportunity. Aggressive safety play is an attempt to make openings. The most aggressive safety shot of all is the deliberate snooker, preferably one of fiendish difficulty. However, leaving the cue ball tight against a cushion with the object ball the length of the table away and not near a pocket is suitably hostile.

Players sometimes adopt safety tactics with an ulterior motive. Finding themselves hopelessly behind in a frame, they nevertheless persist in laying snookers in an attempt to disturb their opponent's potting rhythm. In doing so they hardly improve their own potting rhythm, but if they are feeling out of touch in any case they may feel that they have little to lose.

It is important not to make a fetish of safety play. Treat it as an important aspect of attacking snooker, not as a substitute for it. By all means use it to demoralize your opponents, but not simply to bore them. Your general maxim should be not to use safety for safety's sake, and when you do use it, to do so to the most telling effect.

It would be possible to fill several books with examples of safety tactics, but even then it would only be by chance if some of them directly mirrored actual positions you will face on the table. Such is the infinite variety of snooker. You should, however, find the principles explored in the following examples directly relevant to your own tactical play.

Breaking off

He wide exposure of televised snooker has curbed the appalling practice of playing a power shot on the break off. Even novices now realize that scattering the pack on the opening shot, presumably in the hope of fluking a red, makes a mockery of the game. Almost as foolish, because of its negativity, is the attempt to roll gently into the back of the pack off the top cushion. The player following simply has to return the cue ball to baulk off the top cushion, leaving things more or less as they were before the opening shot. The break-off is a safety shot, and like all safety shots it should be played in a positive manner. If you win the toss, take the opportunity to seize the initiative right from the start.

1 Only novices should break off like this. Aim for the outside red in the last row, playing plain ball with medium strength to bring the cue ball back to baulk off two cushions. The problem with this shot is that the gap between yellow and brown is fairly narrow. A kiss on the brown may leave your opponent with either a potting opportunity or a good chance of being able to leave you near the baulk cushion. Few balls have been disturbed, so the second player is unlikely to be in much difficulty.

2 This is a better way to break off using the same red as 1, and it is regarded by the professionals as the most reliable break-off. Again, aim for the outside red in the last row, but play the shot with running side. This brings the cue ball off both side cushions into the baulk area. The advantage of this shot is that once the cue ball is past the blue it should have an easy path to baulk between the green and the side cushion.

3 This is another shot favoured by the professionals. As in 2, it is played with running side, but in this case it is the outside red of the back row but one that is struck quarter-ball. The cue ball returns to baulk along roughly the same path as 2, the difference being that the last two rows of reds have been disturbed. If you play this shot perfectly it should land your opponent in more trouble than 2, imperfectly and you will leave the cue ball at the top end of the table.

Safety in the early stages

Assuming it has been a successfully executed safety shot, the early stages of a frame should consist of an exchange of safety strokes. This initial sparring continues until a realistic potting opportunity presents itself, either through an error or because the balls are positioned in such a way that it is possible to pick out a ‚shot to nothing' or a plant. As a rule, safety tactics involve putting the maximum distance between cue ball and object ball(s), keeping the latter unpottable. What this means in practice, since the reds are grouped around the top of the table, is getting the cue ball into the baulk area, as close to the baulk cushion as possible. There are exceptions to this, but it is the basis of safety play. The answer to a good safety shot is an even better one. During these early skirmishes you must concentrate fully on making life so difficult for your opponent that it is he, not you, who yields the first opening.

1 Moving the red into the cluster should do no harm, while the natural angle provides a simple route to the safety of the baulk area. Be careful you are not

knocking the first red into others in such a way as to drift one over a pocket.

2 Just clipping the red will take the cue ball off top and side cushions towards baulk. Strive consciously not just to gauge the weight accurately enough to ensure baulk, but to leave the cue ball as close as possible to the cushion. If he has to play with the cue ball right under the cushion, your opponent will find it extremely difficult to return your safety shot with a good one of his own.

3 Clipping the outside red of the cluster is a standard safety shot, because the path back to baulk is uncluttered. But just playing thin off the red, as shown, will leave your opponent in little difficulty.

4 This is an identical situation to 3. Avoid the blue by using running side to widen the angle off the top cushion. Your opponent has a much more difficult safety stroke from this side of the table because the two reds near the side cushion are impeding his path back to baulk.

5 Bearing in mind that the basic objectives of early safety are to get the cue ball near the baulk cushion and/or behind a baulk colour, it is sometimes possible to contrive the kind of shot that sends a loose red towards the pack while screwing down to the baulk cushion with the aid of some left-hand side. To prevent the red returning to the baulk area, play for the pack to catch it like a safety net. This will also disturb a few reds slightly and make your opponent's reply more difficult.

Shots to nothing

The shot to nothing is one of the most valuable tactical

weapons in a snooker player's armoury. In the early stages of a frame in particular, the player who is adept at picking them out and playing them will have a great advantage over the player who sees nothing but potting opportunities on the one hand, and safety strokes on the other. The shot to nothing is one in which a possible pot can be combined with a definite safety stroke. As a rule it means bringing the cue ball safely into baulk, thereby causing no damage should the pot be missed. If the pot succeeds, however, one of the baulk colours can be potted to initiate a break. In the professional game, successful shots to nothing are the most common means of opening the scoring. You will frequently have seen early shots to nothing seal a frame there and then. Doubles and plants are more often than not played as shots to nothing, because of their uncertain outcome, but a great many potting opportunities you might decline can be viewed in a more favourable light when they present themselves as shots to nothing.

1 This is a classic shot to nothing, with the loose red so positioned that the natural angle will see the cue ball safely back to baulk off two cushions. If you make the pot you will almost certainly be on the brown so that you can pot it and get back up the table from it for your next red. If you are unlucky enough not to be on the brown you will be able to snooker behind one of the baulk colours.

2 The same shot as 1 except that, with the brown on its spot, the cue ball has to be left just short of the baulk line to give you a realistic chance of getting a break going. If a player feels positive about the red, he will do this. If he is not, he will be sure to get

the cue ball back to baulk. At the worst, he will then be able to roll up behind a baulk colour. Professionals will invariably play this shot positively.

3 There is just enough room squeeze the loose red through the corridor, while top and side cushion will bring the cue ball back to baulk. You could leave the blue to the middle pocket, but at the worst you can roll behind one of the baulk colours.

4 You have a choice of reds to the middle pocket but if you play the red to the right pocket weight to leave position on the pink, you will be certain to leave your opponent a choice of two reds into the other middle pocket should you miss. However, if you play the red to the left, as shown, stunning gently for the black, you will have prime position if you pot it and will leave nothing if you miss because the main bunch of reds will be shielding the loose ones.

5 Played with screw and right-hand side, the cue ball will run clear of the red near the top cushion, then off both side cushions to finish on the yellow. Judicious use of screw and side will create many shots to nothing.

Choice of shot

You will sometimes face situations in which you have no realistic choice of shot: you must simply take on the pot, regardless of risk, or you must attempt to reach safety by straightforward means. In the course of any frame, however, you will frequently be presented with serious choices, and choosing wisely is obviously vital to your success. Factors like risk and potential reward have to be weighed against each other all the time, while in some circumstances, especially towards the end of a frame, the score itself becomes a prime factor. You must develop the habit of surveying the table closely, rather than allowing yourself to become blinkered by obvious chances. The obvious will frequently be the correct choice, but by no means invariably so, There is no profit whatever in making hasty, impulsive decisions.

1 You have potted the red but failed to get position on a colour. You are presented with a gift snooker simply trickle up behind the yellow. However, consider the brown instead. If you lay your snooker behind it, rather than the yellow, it will be considerably more difficult for your opponent to negotiate an escape route.

2 You want to bring the cue ball to the safety of baulk, and probably the easiest way to do that is by playing thin on the red, which will take the cue ball straight down towards the baulk cushion (A). The trouble is, even if you can leave the cue ball on the baulk cushion, your opponent should be able to return your safety shot. If you play B, however, which is half-ball contact, you put him in far deeper trouble and may actually lay a snooker behind the yellow.

3 Sometimes, two or more reds offer a choice of safety shot. Here you can play safe off Red A with a reasonable possibility of leaving the cue ball safe on the baulk cushion behind the green. Red B, however, is the better option because the yellow and brown are virtually forming a wall. If you can get the cue ball behind it at a certain angle you

have three ball-widths with which to shield the reds.

4 This is undeniably a potting opportunity, but it is one to decline. It is a bad percentage shot. If you were to miss it you might expose yourself to losing the frame. The alternative safety stroke should leave your opponent in some difficulty. It is half-ball contact, doubling the red off two cushions while the cue ball returns to baulk ideally to the baulk cushion behind the brown.

5 If missing a pot guarantees leaving an opening for your opponent, that fact makes the shot appear more difficult than it would otherwise be. For instance, if Red B were not on the table, the pot under consideration would be hazardous, and a thin contact bringing the cue ball back to safety would be advisable. With Red B in position, however, the pot looks altogether more attractive, since there is a fair chance that you will leave the intended red safe if you miss it, with Reds A and B unpottable.

Snookers in the end game

Tactical snookering is applicable at any stage of the game, but when it gets down to the final few reds or, more commonly, the coloured balls alone, the snooker plays a more immediate role. If you are behind in scoring terms by more than the cumulative value of the remaining balls, you must lay one or more successful snookers to have any chance of drawing level or winning. It is tempting for the player ahead by such a potentially decisive margin to adopt 'generous' tactics. In attempting pots, he plays the object ball pocket weight, on the theory that leaving the object ball hanging over the pocket will virtually oblige his opponent to pot it, thereby bringing his own victory one ball nearer. This is flawed theory. If, for example, you are thirty two points ahead with all the colours remaining, your opponent requires two snookers to win. If you allow him to pot yellow, green and brown, he will be twenty three behind, with eighteen points remaining on the table. If he snookers you on the blue, the five-point penalty will leave him in a position to draw level and force a tie-break. If, on the other hand, he pots the blue and snookers you successfully on the pink, the final two balls will steer him to victory. The exception to this cautionary advice is a situation in which you are ahead by a winning margin with only pink and black remaining. Then, of course, pocket weight on the pink will do nicely.

1 With the pink on its spot and the black in a helpful position, there is an excellent chance of laying a snooker behind the black. Try to get the cue ball behind the black and the green behind brown. Use a touch of running side for this shot.

2 The pink and black on their spots leave quite a wide area in the middle of the table to place the blue for a snooker.

3 A three-quarter ball angle on the pink will send it to baulk, while check side should get the cue ball on line for a snooker behind the black.

4 You need a snooker and only the last five colours remain. A gently controlled screw shot should enable you to nestle in behind the brown, but it is even better if you can gauge the pace of the shot to leave the green as near as possible to the back of

the pink. This will of course make the snooker much more difficult to hit. It will also give you every possibility of a free ball or, failing that, a chance to snooker your opponent again.

5 You need a snooker with only the last four colours on the table, but this is an instance where you should think two shots ahead. Rather than play a snooker on the brown, pot it and screw back with right-hand side to leave yourself in prime position to lay the snooker on the blue. If all goes according to plan, you will then be able simply to strike the blue full in the face, killing the cue ball dead with stun to leave it behind the pink with blue doubled off both side cushions towards baulk.

Escaping from snookers

Successfully negotiating a tricky snooker is immensely satisfying as well as important to the result. Of all the situations you will face, this one probably repays the greatest consideration. Bearing in mind that a tactical snooker has a deeper purpose than to extract a few points from you, it is vital that you do not content yourself merely with hitting the object ball. You must hit it in such a manner as not to leave your opponent a scoring opportunity. If you miss it, you must do so in a way that does no more damage than the penalty forfeit. Consequently, it may well be that the easiest or most obvious escape route is not the one to choose a more difficult escape may be less risky overall, even if it increases the chance of a miss . A thorough knowledge of cushion angles is essential to escaping from snookers, and that can only come with experience and careful observation. There is, however, one theoretical point to bear in mind. If the object ball is out in the open, it is sound policy to play a firm shot, so that whether you hit it or not, the cue ball will travel some distance away from it. If the object ball is on or near a cushion, play to roll up to it, because whether you hit or miss, if the balls are close together near the cushion, the object ball should be safe.

1 A straightforward escape using the side cushion. When the object ball is in the open like this, play the shot firmly enough so that if you miss it you will take the cue ball well away from the vicinity.

2 It is difficult to visualize the angle where the first leg is much shorter than the second. Try to imagine the angle as it would appear if the two legs were equal.

3 It would be easier in this case to aim for the cluster of reds, but you would be luckly indeed not leave your opponent with a good potting opportunity. It is better to go for the isolated red, and play with just sufficient strength to reach it. That way, even if you miss, you will not do grave damage.

4 Once escape that occurs time and time again is when you are snookered behind a baulk colour with some but not all reds disturbed from the pack. Your overriding concern here must be safety. Play with dead strength just to reach the pack of reds. Remember that it is better to misjudge the angle slightly to one side— and thus give six away for hitting the pink cause with two open reds your opponent will not have to be a Steve Davis to make at least sixteen easily.

5 This is a nasty snooker because the blue is covering the natural angle on one side cushion, and the

middle pocket the natural angle on the other. Therefore, play it with running side.

6 Whereas object balls in the open should be played at firmly, when they are on or near the cushion you should try to roll up to them, providing, of course, you are not thereby leaving another red. The aim is to leave the cue ball and object ball so close together as to make a pot impossible.

7 With practice, you should become able to escape from relatively simple snookers with a good chance of leaving your opponent very close to the object ball. In this case, leaving him tight against the red would contain the danger even if your opponent again put you in trouble with his next shot.

8 The principal use of swerve is in escaping from a snooker when cushion escapes are blocked.

Safety in the tie-break

Because snooker is a high-scoring game, the issue is usually decided by the time the final black disappears from the table, if not before. Sometimes, however, the frame ends all level. More accurately, the scores are tied with the table cleared, because in snooker the frame is not over until there is a winner. In these circumstances the black is respotted, the players toss for the first shot, and the winner of the toss, plays from the 'D'. However unappetizing that first shot may appear to you, it may pay you to accept it. It is not an easy safety stroke but if it is played well your opponent can be placed in more difficulty than you were. Your own state of mind and confidence—and what you judge your opponent's to be— are relevant factors in this decision.

1 There are alternative ways of playing the opening shot, but this is accepted as standard procedure for attempting an uncomfortable shot. Three-quarter ball across the black, bringing it down to baulk and leaving the cue ball at the top of the table. There are two dangers here: if you hit the cue ball too thick you risk a double-kiss; if you hit it too thin you will leave a pot to the baulk or even the middle pocket.

If the opening shot leaves the cue ball at the top of the table, the second shot is extremely difficult. You must bring the black safely past the middle pocket, while leaving the cue ball as deep as possible in baulk. If the black has not finished as close to the cushion as this, you can play a similar shot to 1, going across the face of the black or doubling it back over the line of the spots.

4

DOWNTURN AND REVIVAL

Once snooker had overtaken billiards in popularity, as it had shortly after the war, billiards faced a long battle for its very survival. There was no professional activity at all between 1951 and 1968 and for much of the later part of the 1960s and early 1970s it seemed as if amateur billiards might peter out similarly. With no professionals setting ultimate standards to strive for and great amateurs like Marshall, Cleary, Wilson Jones, Driffield and Beetham either retiring or passing their peaks, the billiards tradition declined. Billiards remained healthiest not in the British Isles but in other parts of the Commonwealth where the pace of life was slower or where sophisticated professional techniques had been mastered by fewer players. An official coaching scheme might have halted the slide but 'In general the decline of billiards was a sad story of neglect, maladministration and lack of imagination.

The picture was not one of unrelieved gloom, for the period contained players like Norman Dagley, Mohammed Lafir of Sri Lanka, the first player from a junior and unsophisticated billiards nation to win a world title, and Satish Mohan and Michael Ferreira, the two Indians who stood at the head of what had arguably become, in depth, the leading billiards nation.

More nations competed in world amateur championships and players of world class became proportionately more widely spread. The professional championship was again contested minor tournaments sprang up and the general outlook in the late 1970s was certainly much more hopeful than it had been in the early 1960s.

Alf Nolan's English billiards title success in 1964 was to separate two eras rather neatly. From 1949-63, the championship had been won by either Edwards, Driffield or Beetham. Between 1965 and 1984 it was to be won 15 times by Dagley.

Nolan, as English champion, went to New Zealand for the 1964 world amateur championship where Frank Holz, one of the most energetic and capable organisers the game has known since the war, staged the event in his own small country town of Pukekohe. Driffield and Beetham were both invited to go too but the second English place was eventually offered to Karnehm. Wilson Jones, who had just won his ninth Indian title and a newcomer, Michael Ferreira, who had compiled a 353 break in his national championship, represented India. Cleary, who was having difficulties both with his health and his game, was Australia's representative; Francisco, who had made a new South African record of 389 in his 1964 domestic championship, three New Zealanders and a Pakistani, Minoo Mavalwala, completed the field.

Shortly before the event, on September 1, 1964, the B.A. and C.C., with an incredible lack of foresight and without consulting any other nations had drastically altered the rules. By stipulating that the red was always to be replaced on its own spot when potted and by reducing the permitted number of consecutive hazards from 25 to 15 the B.A. and C.C. not only restored a limited version of the spot stroke but removed the incentive for players to master the demandingly skilful top-of-the-table technique based on alternating a cannon with no more than two pots. By making it easier to run up a break with the dull, repetitious and simple spot stroke method as long as a cannon was played every 15th shot a break could continue indefinitely just by potting the red. The players who had mastered the pure top-of-the-table technique were either penalised or forced, to give themselves a better chance of winning, to adopt the spot stroke.

It did take a few months for the implications of the new rule to sink in all their enormity and, as it happened, the Pukekohe event was won by Jones, a player who used it hardly at all. Jones was undefeated but he scraped home by only 144 against young Ferreira and was given a struggle by Karnehm, who did splendidly to finish runner-up. In the latter match, Jones led by only 113 at the interval before three centuries in his first five visits on the resumption gave him a virtually unassailable lead. Jones retired the following year but not before he retained his Indian title. In doing so, he set a new world record of eight centuries in a session.

On his return to England, Karnehm fell to Nolan in the English semifinal but the Geordie was then deprived of his English title by Dagley, who had played out time with 90 unfinished to beat Clive Everton by 11 in the first round before eliminating Driffield in the semi. It is always dramatic when a player wins a major title for the first time, but the way in which Dagley retained the title in 1966 provided one of the most amazing stories in the history of the championship. Groggy after two days in bed with flu, Dagley was outpointed by Nolan by nearly 1,000 on the first day of the final. Feeling better the next day, Dagley overturned these arrears to lead by 49 after five sessions and clinched the match with a 219 unfinished to win by 463.

In 1967, the championship was split into Northern and Southern sections with the Northern at Priory House Social Club, Middlesbrough, and the Southern at Burroughes and Watts, whose takeover by E.J. Riley of Accrington involved the sale of their Soho Square property to the Hurst Park Syndicate and thus the closure of this richly historic match hall, which had been to billiards what Wimbledon's Centre Court is to lawn tennis. It was also to mark the end of the tradition of leading trade firms providing match halls of elegance and distinction. Henceforth, England's leading billiards and snooker events were to be decided in much earthier surroundings.

Dagley looked a good thing for the Southern title but, as had always seemed possible since the partial restoration of the spot stroke, this billiards artist was undone by the concentrated spot stroke assault of Geoffrey Thompson, primarily a snooker player. A break of 368 was the centre piece of Thompson's semifinal win but he was hardly the same player in the final and Everton, who had beaten Karnehm in the other semi, disposed of him quite comfortably.

In the North, Driffield needed a 124 unfinished in the last seven minutes to beat a local hero, Bob Close, by 56 and beat Nolan by a mere 43 in the final. He then proved too consistent and experienced for Everton in the national final at the Albert Hotel, Liverpool, the permanent matchroom of the Liverpool association, which was the kernel of the Lancashire association, a body which in a few years was to exert a dominant influence on the B.A. and C.C.

This entitled Driffield to compete in the 1967 world amateur championship in Colombo. It was fiercely hot and so humid that Driffield and Long both wore cotton gloves on their bridge hands as the only way they could make their cues travel smoothly through their bridges. In his third match, Driffield faced defeat when Francisco, exploiting the spot stroke to the full, made a 301 break to lead by 500 with an hour to go. Driffield rallied with 74 and 127 and, crucially, with a 35-minute 351, and won by 162. After, this he was never in danger, beating Ferreira, who had made the highest break of the event, 507, and the Sri Lankan champion, Mohammed Lafir, at that stage the only other undefeated player, 1,489-726.

Driffield last entered the English championship in 1968 when he was beaten by 141 by Nolan in the Northern semifinal at the Black Swan, Sheffield. Nolan in turn fell to Mark Wildman, who concentrated on the spot stroke so heavily that he potted the red from its spot 107 times in the first two sessions alone. It also loomed large in the 426 break on the second day which was the crucial element in Wildman's 75-point win. Wildman went on to beat Everton by a mere 112 in a low-scoring national final at Almondbury W.M.C., Huddersfield, the loser's path to retaining the Southern title having been smoothed by a car breakdown which caused Dagley to default in the first round. The Southern event was accommodated both in this and the following two years in a basement room in Great Windmill Street, London, which could hold fewer than 40 spectators comfortably. It was a period when it seemed doubtful whether either the Billiards Association or the championship itself would continue to survive.

It was at this nadir of the game's fortunes that Rex Williams, a boys and junior champion nearly 20 years previously, decided to challenge McConachy, now 73, for the world professional billards title which the veteran had held unchallenged since 1951. When he was 16, Williams had made a 510 break which was still his personal best and had also beaten Beetham for the Midland amateur title so his basic technique was extremely sound. Though he had played very little billiards as a professional because there was no public for it Williams never completely forgot it and a snooker tour to Australia gave him the opportunity, backed by a useful sponsorship from John Haig, the whisky distillers, to stop off in Auckland to play McConachy.

The New Zealander's great days were, of course, well in the past but, his cue-arm shaking from Parkinson's disease, he fought with unquenchable spirit to retain his title. In an attempt to control "the shakes" he had adopted ever heavier cues until finally be played with a monster 36 ounce model which, like all his others, he had made himself. Never a fast player, his physical disability and his age made his rate of scoring excruciatingly slow. With gimlet clear eyes shining beneath his characteristic, stiff-peaked, green eyeshield and the fine general physical condition he still maintained with daily running and exercises, McConachy did not wilt until the sixth and final day which he began only 17 behind. The table was much slower and covered with a coarser cloth than Williams was accustomed to factors which helped McConachy's nursery cannons but the scoring was nevertheless disappointing. A break of 293 by Williams in the fourth session was the highest of his seven centuries, none of which were made in the last two days. McConachy made 11 centuries with 236 and 200 as his highest.

Some 8,000 spectators paid to see this almost unique spectacle of a septuagenarian national hero battling with enormous relish for a world title. The standard of play was modest but the epic struggle did at least bring the championship back into circulation.

But what problems were to ensue! Williams, having had the enterprise to challenge and get himself financed, not unreasonably stipulated a £250 guarantee to defend. Fred Davis was nominated as challenger but no British promoter, bearing in mind other promotional expenses and the lack of any proven paying public for billiards, came forward with such a guarantee and his challenge lapsed. This was far from the end of the story, but it was the end for the time being.

A change of chairmanship of the B.A. and C.C. from Harold Phillips to Jack Karnehm led., in September 1968, to a revision of the rules to limit consecutive spot strokes to five. This restored billiards to something much nearer its traditional character. The adoption of Lancashire's proposal that affiliations should be five shillings per club instead of three guineas per league or association aroused bitter opposition but nevertheless put a healthier complexion on the association's finances. It also paved the way for the present system of proportional representation and led to the axis of power swinging from London to the North. Karnehm also arranged for the 1969 World Amateur Billiards Championships to be staged at the Victoria Halls, London, an event which was to expose the association's out of date and inefficient approach by attracting embarrassingly small crowds.

Karnehm, whose suspect temperament had apparently doomed him never to win the English title, earned his place in the championship by beating Thompson by 333 in the Southern final and Wildman by over 1,000 in the national final. Marshall came out of a six-year retirement to win the 1969 Australian title with a top break of 295 and six more over 200, though, as it turned out, his lay-off and the lightning speed of the table which ran seven lengths made him appear a shadow of his former self in London. Ferreira, playing in this third world championship., and Satish Mohan, who made a new Indian record of 584 to beat him for their national title, constituted a strong challenge from India. Francisco, Lafir, the Maltese Paul Mifsud, the Welshman Roy Oriel, and two New Zealanders, Alan Twohill and Frank Holz, made it a record nine nations competing.

The order of play favoured Karnehm, who opened the proceedings with four hours of minimally interrupted practice against Holz prior to tackling Lafir who, as runner-up in Colombo, had some reason to expect a gentler opening match. Karnehm won by 693 and with his next three matches against the players who, with Holz, were to fill the last four places, was able to record five wins while the other fancied contenders were pitched straight into important matches against each other. Karnehm suffered what was to prove his only defeat when Ferreira occupied the last 55 minutes of their first session with 604 unfinished, a world record under the new rules, which he completed to 629 on the resumption. Francisco also had only one defeat against him when he met Karnehm in what was to be the key match. Francisco, who had failed against Driffield in Colombo when he virtually had the match won and who throughout his career was to fall victim to fatal inhibitions when he had chances to amass unassailable leads, was in front for all but a few seconds of the match. Karnehm was also guilty of many bad lapses and it seemed inconceivable, when he trailed by 152 with 17 minutes remaining that he would play out time with 161 unfinished, his only century of the match, to win by nine.

This storybook conclusion for Karnehm undoubtedly strengthened the Englishman's mental fibre for his tests against Marshall and Oriel. He trailed the Australian by 166 with 35 minutes to go but came through with a 62 unfinished to win by 120. Oriel led him narrowly at the interval, but Karnehm was making fewer mistakes and the cornerstone of his technique the in-off game was yielding a consistently high return. He made only four breaks over 200 in the 40 hours he played during the tournament but it was sound, functional and ultimately match winning billiards.

Coming down the final straight, Lafir showed a glimpse of the form which was to give him the world title in Bombay in 1973 when he scored 930 in the first eight visits against Marshall, but Ferreira, on the final day, had to defeat Mohan, and Karnehm had to lose to Wildman to make a play-off necessary. Mohan, though, produced his best display of the championship to beat Ferreira, so Karnehm was already champion when he began his final match.

Karnehm's victory was achieved over a field of a higher overall standard than ever before. Though breaks were much inferior to those world events which featured Marshall, Cleary and Driffield in their—prime and they were playing to more difficult rules—no fewer than eight of the 11 competitors made at least one break over 200. Karnehm's greatest victory was possibly that which he achieved over himself and his temperament. Over a period of many years, no one could have practised harder and few could have kept going in the face of such a persistently extravagant disproportion between his impressive statistics in practice and his unimpressive showings in the English championships.

Shortly afterwards he resigned the chairmanship of the B.A. and C.C. after a stormy period in office. He turned professional and became well regarded as a coach and in the billiard trade through the company of which he was a director, Karnehm and Hillman. In office his dual role as player and administrator exposed him to criticism and it was certainly unfortunate that he should be chairman at a time when Driffield, a member of the council, who had turned professional in October 1968, challenged for the world title in July 1969. Williams was ordered to defend the title within six months but this period elapsed before any proposal was placed before him as to terms or venue. In the meantime, he accepted an offer to defend against Albert Johnson in Australia but the B.A. and C.C. quashed this and insisted that he play Driffield, who at this time was not even a member of the Professional Players Association. At the eleventh hour, it was verbally suggested that Williams should defend against Driffield in the B.A. and C.C.'s new headquarters and match hall at Haringey. He declined and was stripped of the title.

The professionals had a number of disagreements with the B.A. and C.C. or, more specifically, over Karnehm's handling of affairs. They felt strongly that they were not being fairly treated and even that there was a hidden intention for Driffield to play Karnehm for the professional title. So, on December 12, 1970, the P.B.P.A. disaffiliated from the B.A. and C.C., re-formed themselves as the World Professional Billiards and Snooker Association, and declared their autonomy in organising the professional game, a step which immediately dried up all sources of income which the professional game had contributed to the amateur.

The professionals' worst suspicions were confirmed when Driffield and Karnehm duly met for the B.A. and C.C. version of the world title at Middlesbrough Town Hall in June 197 1. Driffield won a farcically easy 9,0294,342 victory. The Middlesbrough Evening Gazette commented: "It is doubtful whether the enthusiasm of the Teesside fans could wear another flop like this even for nothing."

Williams's first defence of the world title under the aegis of the W.P.B.S.A. was also something of a farce. Bernard Bennett, a second-class professional with no substantial previous billiards achievement, fulfilled the conditions set by the W.P.B.S.A. in guaranteeing Williams £250 for a week's title match at Bennett's own club, the Castle in Southampton. Williams displayed his fine top-of-the-table technique in breaks of 480, 372, 325 and 302. Bennett only twice exceeded the hundred.

Eventually, both Driffield and Karnehm, who for some time were the only two professionals to continue to recognise the B.A. and C.C. as the governing body for the professional as well as the amateur game, abandoned this position and became members of the W.P. B.S.A. Driffield never challenged Williams again but Karnehm did so in September 1973 at the Marconi Athletic Club,, Chelmsford, where Williams played some of the finest billiards seen in Britain since the war and dispelled any lingering feeling that he was in any way an unworthy champion. A session average of 217, a match average of 50.7, and a break of 528 as the highest of his 31 centuries were all achieved largely through a top-of-the-table technique so fluent that he made nonsense of the permitted five reds from the spot. From hand he missed only two middle pocket in-offs and one top pocket in-off in the entire match. It was a similar story in Williams's next two defences, both against Eddie Charlton in Australia. At Geraldton in 1974, Williams led by over 1,000 after a day*s play and it was not until the second part of the week, when he won two sessions and made breaks of 488 and 401, that Charlton struck form appropriate to the event. At Geelong in 1976, Williams averaged 121.3 in the ninth session and 65, 67 and 85 in the last three. Charlton succeeded in obtaining high financial guarantees for the matches and without his efforts the championship would have lain dormant. But it was sad that there were no promotional offers for a Williams Davis championship match for Davis as he was to show in 1980 was probably the only professional with the class to threaten the title-holder.

In the amateur game it was undoubtedly the Dagley era for he was to win the English title six times in succession from 1970-75 and the world amateur title at the Malta Hilton in 1971 and at Auckland Town Hall in 1975. A silky-smooth cueist, Dagley attributed much of his success to "being thrashed night after night" by Reg Wright at the Earl Shilton Institute in the depths of Leicestershire. These sessions certainly ingrained in his mind all the correct moves and sequences of shots, the importance of never missing an in-off from hand and the scoring potentialities of top-of-the-table play. Unlike his mentor, however, who often lacked the confidence to play top-of-the-table in matches, Dagley was also blessed with an ice-calm match temperament and a serene faith in his own ability.

He never looked like losing in any of the six English finals. A 467 break featured in his 1970 final against Nolan at Prescot but, unlike Driffield, he had little taste for break-making as such. He tended to produce his best under pressure but it was not all that often that he found himself in this position. After a comfortable retention of the English title in 1971, he started favourite in the World Amateur Championship at the Malta Hilton where the ten competitors were divided into two groups of five with two qualifying from each for a final group of four. Dagley qualified comfortably, as did Mohan, but Ferreira, suffering a crisis of confidence, went out.

In the other group, Mannie Francisco disposed conclusively of all his opponents. Lafir, ill in bed for 30 days before the championship, arrived in Malta late for his first match, carrying only his cue as his luggage had mysteriously gone on to Rome. With his seven stone engulfed in one of the 15-stone Ferreira's shirts, he was pushed straight to the table to play his first match. In the circumstances, he did well to finish second in the group.

In the play-off group, Francisco beat Lafir 1,423-790 before Dagley and Mohan came together for what proved to be the crucial match. Dagley led 927-399 at the interval and by 518 with an hour to go but Mohan, an amazingly quick player with not only good control but a dazzling array of recovery shots, replied with breaks of 192 and 304 with only one scoreless visit between. Dagley, who had reclined in his seat languidly smoking a cigarette as he witnessed his overwhelming lead being reduced to a paltry 24, then made 26 and left Mohan apparently safe, but a brilliant cushion cannon put the Indian in again before he failed at a thin in-off. Supremely calm, as if nothing particular had been happening, Dagley then compiled a completely unruffled 170, his face never betraying anything but faint amusement, to win the match 1,462-1,202. A break of 348 helped Dagley to a 2,014-639 win over Lafir and, with Francisco's earlier form negated by tension, he disposed of the South African 1,565-871 to clinch the title.

The three weeks at the Malta Hilton were also notable for a stormy meeting at which a World Council, a new one nation, one vote body, was formed, initially as the supreme body for World Amateur

Championships but intended also, by some nations, eventually to take over all the international functions of the B. & S.C.C. Traditionally, the B. & S.C.C. had governed the game internationally but it was, in structure and preoccupation, an English domestic body whose meetings were always held in England and attended only by English representatives. Discontent and dissatisfaction had been simmering abroad for some time but the B. & S.C.C. had continued its autocratic line, flourishing a doubtful world copyright on the rules in the faces of other national associations, and reneging on various promises to separate its international and domestic functions.

Overseas nations unanimously condemned the aspect of the B. & S.C.C. constitution which gave Lancashire and Yorkshire alone the voting power to overrule all the other main billiards and snooker nations—even in the unlikely event of them all sending a delegate to the regular meetings in England. But a perhaps misplaced nervousness about upsetting England and a desire to preserve some kind of unity led to a succession of attempted compromises. The World Council was watered down in title to the International Billiards and Snooker Federation and its annual meetings, held to coincide with World Amateur Championships, were generally acrimonious as the progressives grappled with the reactionaries, with those who were simply nervous of change somewhere in between.

Billiards and snooker had outgrown its administration not only on the amateur but on the professional side and all too many officials, instead of considering new ideas in relation to their potential force for progress, reacted to them almost solely in terms of the threat they constituted to their own personal positions.

Though Dagley successfully defended his English title in 1972 and 1973, he competed neither in an unofficial World Open organised by Frank Holz in Pukekohe that year nor, because of eye trouble, in the World Amateur Championship in Bombay in 1973. Driffield, by now a professional,, won the World Open despite losing to both Ferreira and Mohan in round robin play. Mohan finished the round robin undefeated with 11 wins, a 305 break and a 70.8 session average being the best statistics from a series of inspired displays in which his superiority was so pronounced that he had margin for more than a few careless mistakes. But with six to qualify for the concluding knock-out, all Mohan's superiority in the round robin went for naught. Paddy Morgan who., having concentrated on snooker since leaving his native Belfast to turn professional in Australia, played the game of his life, to beat Mohan 21,173-1,719 in the semifinals. Driffield beat Ferreira 1,859-1,678 in the other semifinal and., with Morgan's inspiration lading, won the final comfortably 3,055-2,404.

Though neither Williams, the world professional champion, nor Fred Davis accepted invitations to compete and Dagley was unable to do so, the field was otherwise representative of the strength of both the amateur and professional sides of the game. With all restrictions on amateurs accepting prize money having been abolished in 1971 billiards even more than snooker would have benefited from the regular promotion of official World Open championships, But lack of money and to some extent the unwillingness of certain professionals to risk their reputations against non-professionals—particularly for what they judged to be small rewards—prevented significant progress being made.

Mohan started favourite for the 1973 world amateur title in Bombay but the pressure of home crowd expectation and a certain instability of temperament seemed to weigh crucially not only on him but on Ferreira. They finished second and third behind Lafir, who was twice the player in 90° that he had been in Malta or New Zealand, where in 70° he had worn a pullover under his shirt and waistcoat and still had hands like blocks of ice. In the 1974 World Amateur Snooker Championship, in a Dublin winter, he was reduced to huddling over a portable gas fire between shots, warming his hands on a cup of coffee. Bombay removed not only this problem but that of diet, for his eating during visits to the Western world had to be largely confined to the hot tasting and strong smelling dried fish he carried with him in a glass jar.

He also received significant assistance from his great friend, Bert Demarco, the Scotsman who, some six months before the 1973 championship, gave him the crucial gift of a set of billiard balls. The previous year the Composition Billiard Ball Supply Co., whose association with the B. & S.C.C. had, in effect, given them a ball monopoly, announced that they were discontinuing the manufacture of crystalate, the championship ball, in favour of a new ball, the super crystalate. The B. & S.C.C. tamely accepted this and the new ball was adopted for all recognised championships.

There were teething problems: an extra coating of high lustre finish was discontinued when it was found to be contributing to an unpredictably wide "throw" of the cue-ball in certain shots and to an unusual number of "kicks". Snooker playérs tended to welcome the greater ease with which screw shots could be executed and the new ball tended to make big breaks easier to compile, but billiards players proved much more reluctant to accept it, chiefly because, even with out the high lustre finish, it tended to be less predictable than the old. To countries with foreign exchange difficulties one problem posed by the adoption of the new ball was simply that of availability. Demarco's gift provided l,afir with what was until after the championship the only set of super crystalate balls in Sri Lanka.

Lafir, who had learnt to play billiards on his family dining table, using a broomstick for cue, marbles for balls, a sarong for cloth and a cycle tube for cushions, had other worries. The government had recently banned horse racing so his job as a commission agent had, in one of his characteristically picturesque phrases, "gone for a walk". Having no money of his own and a family to support, Lafir lived on £50 which Demarco had sent him and miscellaneous help from friends. When he compiled 27 breaks over 500 in the six months before the championship, it was clear he had a great chance to win but it was only by 14 that he scraped home against Everton, the Welsh champion, In a desperate finish in his first match. Lafir then beat Ferreira by 386 and rewarded his friend Demarco, his next opponent, for all his help by amassing a new world amateur record aggregate for four hours of 2,850 with breaks of 428,

404- 318 and 302. With Mohan beating Ferreira by 158, he and Lafir were the only undefeated players when they met on the 11th day in front of a capacity crowd with hundreds turned away. Lafir led by 420 at the interval but added only 11 in his first five visits after the resumption, Mohan halved the gap but Lafir came to life with 394 and with three further centuries and a 350 unfinished, triumphantly averaged, 71.5 to win 2,213-1,079. Playing with supreme confidence, Lafir then smashed the world amateur break record with an 859 against Eric Simons, almost all of it postman's knock, in 49 minutes 47 seconds, before he missed a middle pocket pot red from the spot end with position lost.

Mohan kept in pursuit by beating Philip Tarrant, the best Australian since the legendary Marshall, Cleary and Long, but once Lafir had also beaten Tarrant by 494 the championship was virtually his. Ultimately his last match proved irrelevant as Everton surprisingly beat Mohan by 128 to leave Lafir in an unassailable position.

In Britain Dagley's reign continued. Nolan, 125 behind with 13 minutes to go, pipped Everton by 19 in the 1974 English semifinal and made a great effort in the last session of the final, reducing his arrears from 503 to 196 with 45 minutes to go before Dagley again trod on the accelerator. This capacity to pluck out a break when he needed it was again in evidence in the 1975 final when Bob Close, playing in front of his highly partisan supporters in his own club, Western Social, Middlesbrough, followed his semifinal win over an off-colour Nolan by making his highest competitive break to date, 217, in reducing Dagley's lead of 437 to only two with 40 minutes left. At this stage Close, in attempting a very thin in-off white, sent his cue-ball straight into the pocket a—foul stroke under a rule amendment of 1972 prohibiting misses except when the striker was in hand and no ball out of baulk. Electing to have the balls spotted, Dagley compiled a 117 and went away to win by 224.

Dagley and Close thus travelled as England's representatives in the World Amateur Championship in New Zealand in September 1975. Dagley was never in the slightest danger in his group, in which he recorded breaks of 300, 348, 374 and 477, while the second qualifier was David Sneddon, an inexperienced but fast and very determined Scot who beat the Indian no. 2, Girish Parikh by 59 in the vital match. Ferreira who, earlier that year, with Mohan having emigrated to Australia, had set a world record session average of 128.4 and a record match average of 69.7 in the Indian championship, topped the second group. Everton took Wales into the semi-finals by beating Close by 363 after the Englishman had gained a bizarre win over Long, who produced the barest shadow of the form of his great days. With five minutes to go, Long led by 20 with perfect top-of-the-table position only to nervously drop his cue on the cue-ball; then, 22 behind but still with time to win, Long dropped the cue-ball under the table and wasted precious seconds ferreting it out. He was still in play, nine short, when the bell rang.

Dagley and Ferreira both won their semifinals easily, Ferreira perhaps too easily for he made six centuries in each session for an average of 50.4. The key to the final, after the Indian had led by eight at the first interval, was the second of the four sessions, for

Dagley took a small unfinished break to 200 and made it three double centuries in as many visits with further contributions of 228 and 202 in a 47 minute spell which destroyed Ferreira's touch and fluency. Ferreira made a slight recovery but there was no keeping Dagley from his second world title.

There seemed nothing to prevent Dagley from increasing his total of English title successes to a record nine but Everton, in the same year that he took his fourth Welsh title, played the game of his life to beat him by 83 in the semifinal in Middlesbrough, a 61.1 second session average proving the crucial statistic. Reaction set in the final, however, for after Everton's 287 break in the opening session and a lead of 333 early in the second, Close replied with a lifetime highest break in competition of 259 and gradually pulled the match round to win by 219.

A similar thing happened in 1977 when Beetham, a veteran of 67, dipped into his past to produce his best performance for years to beat Dagley by 76 in the quarterfinal before beating Everton by 197 in the semi and fading against Close in the final.

At the end of the year, Close reached a new personal peak by eliminating Dagley in the six hour semifinal of the World Amateur Championship in Melbourne. Even five centuries and a 99 in one of his group matches against David Pratt did not fully prepare pundits for a first session against Dagley in which he made a 234 and four other centuries to finish 519 ahead. He extended his lead to 701 but Dagley made a great effort to narrow the gap to 180 with 15 minutes to go before he ran out of time. In the other semifinal, Ferreira comfortably disposed of Everton who, having displaced a joint in his back two days before the championship, had achieved second place in Dagley's group despite severe pain and a makeshift stance. Ferreira, who had made a break of 519 and six more over 300 in winning each of his five group matches, had nevertheless looked vulnerable under pressure and was perhaps fortunate, in the eight-hour final, that Close had expended precious reserves of nervous energy in beating Dagley.

Though Close made the early running, with the highest break of the match, 231, and led by 249 at one point. Ferreira gradually gained confidence to start the final period with a 323 advantage. However, the Englishman's determination combined with the Indian's insecurity within sight of victory to produce a thrilling finish, Close getting to within 26 before the Indian, whose highest break in the final session was a paltry 70, virtually fell over the line to win by 119. Ironically, Ferreira's form in winning the title—he averaged only 20.8 in the final—had been much inferior to that he had often shown in championships in which ultimate success had eluded him. There was, at the best, however, a fluency, certainty and speed which bore witness to the intensive practice and preparation which he would have found impossible to sustain without his deep love of, and dedication to, the game.

He immediately went to Christchurch, New Zealand, for an unofficial World Open organised by Frank Holz and won this also, surviving a close semifinal by a mere 82 against his compatriot Parikh. He then set a new world amateur session average record of 189.8—the 1,709 session total included breaks of 333, 239, 347, 515 and 190 unfinished in the final in beating Wildman, who, after what he described as "seven years in the wilderness", had played his best competitive billiards for years, 3,461—1,309.

It was a tournament which emphasised again, through its high general standard, the need to work towards official World Open championships as a way of sustaining competitive interest for, with no new challenger on the horizon, Williams continued to hold the world professional title unopposed. It also underlined the fact that leading players were making such liberal use of the "five pots from the spot" rule that breaks were escalating, perhaps to an unacceptable level. Big breaks made by repetitive stroke sequences had always damaged billiards as a public spectacle, notoriously through the nursery cannon specialists of the 1930s, and fears that the game's modest revival might be hindered if breaks again grew too large began to be expressed. Almost all leading players were part of a groundswell of opinion that consecutive pots from the spot should be limited to two or at most three.

5

THE CHANGING ORDER

Billiards progressively regained its distinctive character and appeal as the "five consecutive pots from the spot" rule was amended first to three and then to two. The International Billiards and Snooker Federation, which had in effect assumed responsibility for the rules when the Billiards and Snooker Control Council undertook not to make any change without consulting this one-nation, one-vote body, agreed in November 1978, that from the following January there would be a reduction from five to three. In August, 1978, unilaterally and precipitately, the four authentic professional billiards players, Rex Williams, Fred Davis, John Barrie and Jack Karnehin recommended and the W.P. B. S.A. main board approved—that all professional matches would be played under the two-pot rule.

This effectively scuppered a new £2,000 British Open proposed by Jim Williamson for his Northern Snooker Centre in Leeds. Instead, Williamson mounted a revival of the United Kingdom Professional Championship under the sponsorship of Super Crystalate. Williams started desperately badly against Ray Edmonds in the quarter-finals and trailed 165-599 but, only three visits from the end, made a break of 309 to win this five-hour match by 1,557-1,350. He then beat Karnehm and Barrie, both relatively comfortably, to win the £1,000 first prize. Barrie made the highest break, 444, in beating Davis in the other semi-final.

On the amateur front, the period between 1978 and 1983 continued to be internationally dominated by Michael Ferreira, a Bombay lawyer., and Dagley, manager of a Nuneaton snooker centre. In this time, Dagley reached two finals and two semi-finals but did not add to the two world amateur titles he won in Malta in 1971 and Auckland in 1975. Ferreira, who had won in Melbourne in 1977, won twice more, in Delhi in 1981 and in Malta in 1983, to leave only the veteran Australian Robert Marshall, with four titles, as a more prolific winner of the event. Ferreira was always conscious of the record book and became, through the hard practice he allied to a naturally quick eye, a superbly fast and fluent break-maker even though he remained unduly vulnerable under pressure for a player of his ability. Dagley lacked Ferreira's insatiable appetite for breaks but almost always responded positively to pressure until twice defeated by Ferreira in extraordinary matches in the final of the 1981 world amateur and the semi-final two years later.

Ferreira tolled the passing of the five-pot rule with five world records in the 1978 final of the Indian championship. In the first session, he made a break of 1,149—superseding Dagley's 862 in the English championship earlier that year and in the second he made breaks of 611, 259 and 995, missing a six-inch pot red to conclude the latter as he was rushing in the last few seconds to make his second thousand. This second session produced a record aggregate of 1,949 and a session average of 243.6. His four-hour aggregate,

3,317, and 157.9 average were also records under these rules though, under the more stringent two-pot rule, Marshall had recorded a 3,391 four-hour total.

Dagley retained the English title in 1979, making three triple centuries on the first day against a new finalist, Ken Shirley. With Middlesbrough engulfed by snow, the electricity supply proved inadequate on the second day and only four bouts of play were possible, giving 2 hr 19 min. less than the designated five hours. With Shirley due back at the wheel of his police car next day he was the first to agree, trailing by 1,762 points, that Dagley should be declared the winner.

Ferreira took first place over Dagley, Barrie, Karnehm and Lafir in a five-man round robin at Bombay Gymkhana, but crowds were thin and the highest break was only 332 by Barrie, always the English gentleman in waistcoat and tie in the broiling heat. Neither did Dagley prosper in the tropics when the World Amateur Championship was staged in Colombo. His tip flew off 40 minutes into his first match against the rising Indian no. 2, Subash Agrawal, to whom he iost by 279. This was his only defeat in his group, from which he and Paul Mifsud went through on points difference at the expense of Agrawal. As expected, Ferreira and Lafir qualified from the other group, though Lafir was clearly not the player he had been in winning the title six years previously, when he last appeared in the event, and Dagley beat him easily in the semi-finals.

Mifsud was a rank outsider against Ferreira. He had arrived from Malta only ten hours before his first match after being delayed 24 hours in Paris and 26 in Bombay but with superb potting, a sound inoff game and excellent control in long runs of postman's knock at the top of the table, he had already improved beyond recognition on any previous billiards showing. Nevertheless, he seemed to be fading out quietly when he trailed Ferreira by 618 midway through the middle session. In pointing out a speck of dirt, Mifisud inadvertently touched the ball. Ferreira, quite correctly, claimed a foul but Mifsud was so incensed that he banged the balls about aimlessly for a few minutes. Ferreira lost his concentration and suddenly Mifsud, controlling his anger, made breaks of 338 and 153 to trail by only 183 going into the final session. Ferreira cracked completely and Mifsud won 21,489-1,856.

Dagley had a truly appalling run of the balls in the opening session of the final and averaged a meagre 8.9. He could not get going in the second session either but was still only 464 behind until Mifsud, with impeccable timing, played out with 359 to lead by a daunting 823 overnight. Mifsud added only two to his unfinished break but no counter attack came from Dagley as a final score of 2,943-2,152 gave Malta its first sporting world champion.

Preferring snooker, Mifsud did not play competitive billiards again. His hopes of holding both world amateur titles simultaneously were thwarted by Jimmy White, 8-6, in the snooker semifinals in Launceston, Tasmania, in 1980, and he was beaten 5-2 by the Canadian Jim Bear in the 1982 quarterfinals in Calgary. He played professionally for two seasons, reaching 48th place in the snooker rankings, but the strain of commuting from Malta to Britain and the separations from his father and friends prompted him to relinquish his professional status. Returning to top level competition., he won the World Amateur Snooker Championship in Blackpool in 1985, to complete a unique double of world billiards and snooker titles.

After his Colombo disappointment, Dagley was given a twinge of anxiety by Everton in the 1980 English final trailing by 363 midway through the penultimate session before breaks of 506, 299 and 352 within five visits gave him a record 111.4 average for the 2½-hour session as he went on to win 2,825-2,172.

The second Super Crystalate UK Professional championship at Leeds that year provided a surprise win for Karnehm, whose solid basic billiards with a strong emphasis on in-offs prevailed over a fitful Williams, who snatched the lead in the third session with a break of 423, after trailing by 501 overnight, before Karnehm's consistency saw him home 2,518-2,423.

Commercial reality demanded that he concentrate on snooker, though he did return to his first love to win the UK Championship in 1951, beating the ageing Willie Smith and Kennerley, and was invariably able to play entertainingly in the half-hour or so of billiards with which he liked to commence his exhibitions. His friendship with Williams, with whom he made many exhibition tours for Watneys, the brewers, discouraged him from pursuing the billiards title in the Seventies, particularly as there was always the problem of finding a promoter who could assemble a satisfactory deal. Almost concurrently, his friendship with Williams cooled when they found themselves on opposite sides in the snooker world's political squabbles just as Williamson arranged for the Yorkshire Bank to become the chief sponsors of the Leeds title promotion which enabled him to guarantee £1,500 for the winner and £1,000 for the loser of the four day match.

Adding to the emotion of the world championship, Willie Smith, by now 94 and almost blind, made a rare excursion from his Leeds home to witness the final session and present the trophy. As he sat in his seat of honour opposite the red spot, the click of the balls and the tones of the referee acted like the smell of the greasepaint to this rare old character, still full of wit and reminiscence.

One anecdote went back almost 70 years to his days touring with Diggle when he shared a room with this great eccentric. Diggle, obsessed with the idea that someone was following him, not only developed a nervous habit of continually looking behind him but carried a revolver to cover all eventualities. One night, the dozing Smith became aware of Diggle waking abruptly and sitting bolt upright in bed.

"They're coming, Willie," he shouted, fired a shot through the door and fell back asleep. Smith, who had said of snooker of its early days: "If the public will stand for this they'll stand for anything," had just watched television coverage of the Embassy World Championship. He admitted that he had enjoyed it but added with an impish, oblique reference to all the wrangles over rules in which he had participated in his heyday: "I'd have enjoyed it a lot more if they'd changed the rules."

"Which rules?"

"'All of them."

Prior to Smith's arrival for the final session, Davis had outpointed Williams by more than enough to assure himself of victory. The second day, during which his highest break in the five hours' play was 71, was particularly disastrous for the champion. With a nice sense of theatre, Davis began the final session by carrying an unfinished break of 62 to 583, the highest in the championship for 46 years. His 5,978-4,452 win made him the only player, except his elder brother, to win both world professional titles. "This was a special incentive," he admitted.

Less than six months later, Davis retained the title at the Brownsver Hall Hotel, Rugby, when a prize fund of £8,300, including £4,000 for the winner, guaranteed by Ivan Cawood, a Rugby estate agent, enabled the event to return to a tournament format for the first time since 1934. The challenge system, as the history of the game had shown all too clearly, had made it possible for the champion to delay or even evade challenges by protracting negotiations or imposing impossible conditions. Its passing was unlamented, not least by Mark Wildman and Ray Edmonds, who made their first impacts on professional billiards in this 11-man event. Edmonds beat Karnehm in the quarterfinals, the first of three consecutive occasions he was to do so in this tournament, and Wildman remarkably beat Williams 1,476-1,415 after Williams's break of 517 had given him a commanding 762-148 lead. Wildman beat Edmonds comfortably in the semifinals, but had nothing left for the final in which Davis led from gun to tape to win 3,037-2,064.

With Cawood again guaranteeing the prize fund, Williams pocketed the £2,750 champion's cheque in the Super Crystalate UK but Margate in February was not a location to provide much gate money. Throughout the competition Williams played beautifully, making breaks of 505 in beating Davis 2,003 999 in the semifinals, and 393 and 385 in overcoming Karnehm 1,592-1,112 in the final. Karnehm had earlier excelled himself with a break of 390 to beat John Barrie 1,338-1,074 in their semifinal after trailing by 183 with 35 minutes to play.

In the early summer of 1981, Edmonds not only won the billiards event at the Guinness billiards and snooker festival on the Isle of Wight from a field which included Dagley, Ferreira and Charlton but also another £1,000 first prize from the Midas Masters. The Midas event was as poorly attended at Margate as the UK had been, but the experiment of introducing matches of either the best of seven or best of nine games of 200 up, pointed the direction in which billiards had to proceed if it was to have any real potential as a television attraction. Soon after, Cawood, who had also underwritten the Midas event, retired from the fray nursing his financial bruises.

From television's point of view, the traditional match formats of billiards—either a specified number of playing hours or a single game to a points target—did not possess the recurrent crises on which the medium thrives. Snooker, with each frame containing its own crisis within a larger structure of the match, is ideal for television in this respect and the prevailing opinion of the billiards world, against the aesthetic instincts of most of the players, moved towards the necessity of adapting to the demands of the age. The choice lay starkly between keeping championship billiards within a knowledgeable little world of its own or attempting modifications of format with which it might interest a wider public. Another necessary ingredient for enhancing public interest was top-class new recruits to the professional ranks, but the amateur champion Dagley was not yet convinced that a billiards revival, despite a few encouraging signs, could be maintained. Because of his fondness for biennial overseas trips to world championships, he delayed turning professional, and without much difficulty cruised into the final of the 1981 World Amateur Championship at the Sheraton Hotel, Delhi. Ferreira was statistically even more impressive, setting new world amateur session and match average records of 191.8 and 123.6 against Bob Close in his last group match and making a 630 break, also a record under the three pot rule, in submerging his talented compatriot Agrawal 3,272-1,964 in their semi-final.

Billiards had for a long time enjoyed a high sporting profile in India, and Ferreira, by now ensconced in a job which left him free to concentrate on the game as much as he wished, was a national sporting hero, a status which appeared to rule out turning professional, It is difficult to imagine anywhere but in India 1,400 spectators watching the last of the four sessions of the final, which Ferreira began with a lead of 545. With 40 minutes to play, Dagley had reduced the gap to 46 but Ferreira steadied himself admirably to compile a break of 244. The great escapologist looked as if he might still do it as he ran up 182 but with four minutes remaining, just enough time to overturn an 88-point deficit, he left himself in a cover at the top of the table.

Two years later, Ferreira retained the title by comfortably defeating Agrawal in Cospicua, Malta, but the key to his success was an incredible semifinal victory over Dagley, who led him by no fewer than 735 going into the final session. Ferreira had made only one century in two sessions but in making a break of 463 and three single centuries he cast all inhibitions aside to average 99 and win by 64. The W.P.B.S.A. officially supported billiards for the first time when it contributed £2,000 to the £8,000 prize fund for the 1983 World Professional championship at the La Reserve Club, Sutton Coldfield. The championship fund also included £5,000 from Ansells, the brewers, secured as a goodwill gesture for this new snooker centre, and £1,000 from Hainsworth, the cloth manufacturers. The match statistics were poor largely because the pockets on the match table were found to be fully 1/8 in, narrower than standard. On regaining the title, Williams said: "If the pockets are too tight, the shape and pattern of the game changes. This destroys the confidence of the players and makes them take alternative shots so that they lose position."

These difficulties and the change of match format from time limit to points target produced some long matches, notably Williams's 1,500-1,494 victory over Davis in the semi-finals. Needing 20, Williams missed an in-off, Davis, needing 78, reached 72 before running slightly out of position and missing a cushion cannon by a whisker. Williams beat Wildman easily in the last two-day final deemed appropriate for the modern game.

With four-session match averages of 55.6 and 51.3 in the last two rounds, Dagley won his 13th English amateur title in 1982, but Ferreira, despite a new four-hour aggregate record of 3,059 in an early round, was beaten by an outstanding 20-year-old prospect, Geet Sethi, in the Indian championship. Sethi secured the title by beating Agrawal through turning a 400-point deficit with 75 minutes to play into a 2,269-1,350 win with breaks of 188, 140, 277, 271 and 544 in this period. Three years later Sethi was to win the world title.

A future world professional champion made his first impact almost at the same time. Robbie Foldvari, a 22-year-old protege of Murt O'Donoghue, from whom he absorbed a very sound top-of-the-table technique, won the first of his two Australian amateur titles by defeating George Gamin junior, champion for the preceding six years.

In the professional game, Wildman broke through to win the 1983 UK championship at the Victoria Snooker Centre, Southend. Having won the British under-16 and under-19 titles at both billiards and snooker in the Fifties, he did not really achieve his potential in an amateur career of which the highlight was the 1968 English billiards title. Partly through a somewhat mercurial temperament, partly because of his career as an area manager with United Dominions Trust, the city finance house, he spent almost a decade in the wilderness, achieving very little, but on turning professional in 1980 he started to score some useful wins at snooker, notably over Perrie Mans and John Spencer, and reached two world billiards finals.

A player of purple patches, between whose worst and whose best there was a wider gap than is usual with most players of his class, he overturned a 616-750 interval deficit against Williams in the semi-finals of the UK championship with a break of 495, a lifetime best, and a session average of 98.2 to win 1,500-1,272.

He trailed Davis 477-750 at the interval of the final but the veteran, then 69, collapsed in the final session, making a top break of only 43 as Wildman won 1,500-1,032. On this form, Wildman appeared to have every chance of winning the world professional title at the Court Snooker Centre, Peterborough, of which he was the co-proprietor, but the extra strains and stresses of being involved in the promotion unhinged his game completely as he fell to Chariton in the quarterfinals 1,500-778.

Far more sensational and far reaching in its effects, however, was an incident on semifinals day when Williams arrived at the venue during the first session of the Davis v. Charlton match. He asked to practise on a table situated on a balcony above the arena but, in line with a refusal given to another competitor earlier in the week, permission was denied on the grounds that it might disturb the concentration of the players. Williams stomped angrily out of the club and was still missing when his semifinal with Edmonds was due to start at 1.30 though, as it happened, Davis and Charlton overran and the second semifinal was not ready to start until 1.48.

Although it is solely the player's responsibility to appear on time, club officials phoned Williams at his hotel. Williams said that he would be at the club in half an hour and the match actually started at 2.36. Edmonds seethed and Wildman, as promoter, and the two tournament referees, Bob Sconce and Mike Clark, both caught the sharp edge of Williams's tongue. Edmonds, Wildman and Sconce all submitted official complaints to the W.P.B.S.A. and after a 2¼-hour discussion Williams was fined £500. Williams, who had been chairman of the W.P.B.S.A. for eight of the preceding 14 years, resigned as soon as the decision was announced but remained a member of the board. He said: "I have played my last billiards match. I don't need all that aggravation." Two months later, he was re-installed as chairman.

Strangely, the aggravation, entirely of his own making, did not prevent him from averaging 60 against Edmonds in the semifinal and from overwhelming Davis so completely in the final, 1,500-605, that Anglia TV, persuaded to cover billiards for the first time, found the play too repetitious and undramatic to renew their interest. It was thus made unmistakably clear that billiards, in a traditional format, was a non-runner for television. From the prize fund of £8,000, of which £5,000 was provided by the W.P.B.S.A., Williams took £3,000 as champion but his retirement from billiards threatened to devalue the championship just as the non-entry of John Roberts junior, Melbourne Inman, Willie Smith and Walter Lindrum all had in their time.

Billiards also lost ground through no promoter or sponsor coming forward for the UK. Even the World Professional Championship looked like falling into limbo until, with less than three months to spare, an £8,000 prize fund was assembled for 1984. Strachans, the cloth manufacturers, supplied £3,000 as main sponsors with the Majestic Snooker Club, Portsmouth, and the W.P.B.S.A. contributing £2,500 each. Williams not only stood out of the event but did it a disservice in stating to the Daily Star: "Whoever wins the championship at Portsmouth can play me over three days for whatever sum of money he wants to see who really is the billiards champion of the world." A reversion to the time limit system after the late-night marathons in 1983 produced some dramatic finishes. Charlton played out time with 92 to beat Karnehm by 13 in the quarterfinals', but from 87 behind with eight minutes of the final remaining, the Australian could make only 54 to leave Wildman the new champion by a mere 33 points. Ironically, in view of the previous year's experience, the last half-hour of the final would have made very dramatic television viewing as Wildman came under pressure. As his winning average of 19.7 implies, the standard of play was modest but the championship had been maintained as a going concern and within two years was to have television coverage.

In 1985, the W.P.B.S.A., flush with cash from its snooker contracts, guaranteed a £20,000 prize fund for the billiards championship rising by annual increments to £30,000 by 1990. This made the future of the event more secure than ever before and prompted Dagley and, a year later, Close to turn professional.

Dagley's valedictory performance in the amateur ranks, the 1984 English final at Widnes, saw him turn his 347 deficit against Close halfway through the penultimate session into a 351 interval lead with breaks of 303, 156 and 177 unfinished. He made only ten visits in the final session in scoring 1,477 for an average of 147.7, a new record under the two-pot rule. His last three visits as an amateur brought him breaks of 401, 472 and 280 unfinished as he clinched his 15th English amateur title.

There were three new amateur records in an invitation tournament in India, at B.C.A. Garware, as

Agrawal made a break of 716 to supersede Foldvari's 615 in the Victoria championship in November., 1983, and aggregates of 1,854 and 3,485.

Statistical considerations aside, more interesting developments were afoot as Channel 4, eager to make a reputation for covering sports new to television., agreed to seven one-hour billiards programmes. "Straight" billiards was rejected on the grounds that the event might not be dramatic enough for a non-specialist audience. Various formats were considered and the one adopted was that of the best of three half-hour games—with the significant proviso that no player could occupy the table for more than 15 minutes in any half-hour game. The billiards world felt that this did not differ any more from "real" billiards than did limited overs from "real" cricket. Williams emerged from billiards retirement to win the event, the Blue Arrow Masters, and audiences varied between 5.67 m. and 2.11 m., extremely satisfactory figures.

The BBC did not confirm their tentative offer to cover the World Professional Championship final at Hatton Garden Snooker Centre, London, but the W.P.B.S.A.'s billiards committee nevertheless stood by its decision, conditioned but not determined by the prospect of television coverage, to make the championship Matches the best of five games of 400 up. The new format suited Edmonds down to the ground as he beat Wildman 3-0 in the semifinals and Dagley 3-1 in the final to take the 0,500 first prize. The final would have made riveting television: Edmonds ran out with 30 to win the first game by a mere five; Dagley won the second in ten visits 400-307; Edmonds the third 400-315, running out with 140 unfinished. In what proved to be the clinching game, Edmonds missed an easy cannon when needing only 19 and Dagley, at his last chance, ran 110 before breaking down within 14 of game.

With Dagley out of the way, Close won his third English title in appalling conditions at Chester to qualify for the World Amateur Championship but three of the four semifinalists at the Taj Hotel, Delhi, were Indians and the fourth, remarkably, was Robert Marshall who, at the age of 75, had emerged from a 15-year retirement earlier in 1985 to win his 20th Australian amateur title. None of his statistics in that event promised a serious challenge in Delhi, where Ferreira hoped to emulate Marshall's record of four titles but where the veteran himself astonishingly came within one match of winning his fifth.

An arthritis sufferer, Marshall had within the last two years been fitted with a steel pin in his hip and a steel plate in his right knee. An operation to remove a nonmalignant melanoma from his back had placed extra strain on his shoulder and cueing arm. But as his cue arm grew stronger, all the knowledge and touch in his brain was brought out by practice. In Delhi, he made two triple centuries and twice scored five centuries in a session, beating Ferreira and all other opponents in his group.

Ferreira finished second in this section only by beating Latif Amir Bux, the best player Pakistan has produced, by a mere three points after trailing by 46 with only four minutes to play. Bux, who had lost by only 22 to Marshall, was an unlucky third. In the other group, the two Indians provided a feast of breaks, including 512 and 599 from Agrawal and 563 and 604 from Sethi. Agrawal also set a new 3,780 four-hour aggregate record against the Maltese Alf Micallef, making 15 centuries in the match, nine of them in the second session, in which he totalled 2,224 for an average of 92.6. Agrawal appeared burnt out in losing his semifinal to Marshall by 890. Sethi trailed Ferreira by 555 going into the final session, but closed the gap with 187 and 303, and then scored 125 and 74 at his last two visits to win by 134.

Showing signs both of reaction from this win and of stress from being in the final, Sethi struggled in his first session against Marshall but the veteran Australian missed his chance to take a commanding lead and led by only 223 at the first interval. In the second session, Sethi overcame his nerves as he took the lead with a break of 446 and added 235 and 225 unfinished in averaging 90.3 to lead by 539 at halfway. He doubled this lead to 1,166 in the third session and the last two hours was a formality.

6

CUE CONTROL AND CUE BALL CONTROL

Anyone who has spent any time at all on a snooker table knows that it is easy enough to pot a red ball now and again. And if that pot leaves the cue ball well positioned on a colour, either by luck or intention, there is a good chance of knocking in the colour as well. In other words, even on the first occasion you picked up a cue it is virtually certain that you managed to pot a few reds, and quite likely that you managed the two ball sequence of red followed by colour, which is of course the cornerstone of the game. Those two balls represented a break whether made by you in the course of your initiation or by Steve Davis on his way to another tournament victory.

If that is so, why is it a matter of common observation that the game is technically so difficult? Along with billiards it is probably the most technically difficult game ever devised. You know that, whether you are a novice, a casual club player or a good amateur. Millions who watch the game on television know that, including the large proportion who have never been near a table. The top professionals are never allowed to forget it.

The obvious strain the pros are under at critical moments in a vital frame is not caused by the TV lights and cameras, which most of them have lived with for so long that they seem normal furniture. Nor, as is frequently assumed, does it stem from the fact that the financial stakes are high. No one ever made a match-winning break with his mind on his bank balance. Nor is it simply that losing to a rival is a distasteful experience, to be avoided if at all possible. It feels better to win than to lose, but that universal emotion applies at club level as much as it does at the top. No, the principal reason for the strain, for the intense concentration of the players, and the palpable tension amongst the live audience and in front of millions of TV screens, is that the players are trying to do something very difficult. They know what to do and they know how to do it. All they have to do is strike the cue ball exactly right a purely technical matter. If they do it they will succeed. If they do not they will fail.

The fundamental skill

Striking the cue ball exactly right is what snooker is all about. Striking it right not just now and again, which anyone can do, but again, and again and again.

That may sound like a gross oversimplification, but a moment's reflection will tell you that it is not. In order to achieve any desired result with the object ball and subsequently with the cue ball, you simply have to strike the cue ball at the correct point, on the correct line and with the correct strength, The correct lines ensures the pot, while the other two factors determine the position on the table at which the cue ball will come to rest. The skills involved in doing this are in varying degrees the finer points of snooker. Do not, however, even think of proceeding to that chapter until you have studied the present one. Until, indeed, you have absorbed the information here and incorporated it into your play. And that warning is directed at the club player of good standard as much as it is at the novice. The key to successful snooker is the cue action. There is an exact parallel here with golf. It is plain to anyone that the action of the golf swing itself far outweighs any other aspect of the game, Choosing the right shot and the right club for it are simple matters, which is why when you watch Ballesteros on television you almost invariably know what he is trying to do. But the swing! That damnable swing! It is the curse of the Sunday golfer, and the bane of the professional's life. In both cases they practise it endlessly. They never doubt for a moment that if their swing is on song, the game will follow; that if it is not, all is in vain.

The key to success

For some curious reason, run-of-the-mill and even quite good snooker players do not have a similar obsession with their cueing action. They worry about potting angles and gaining position. They strive to gain cue ball control by the use of spin, so that they can move remorselessly from ball to ball, just as their idols do on television. They strive to turn their twenty breaks into forty breaks, and maybe in their wildest dreams they think the magical century break may one day come their way. Months and even years go by and they advance little beyond a rudimentary standard of play. Why? They understand the tactics of the game perfectly well these may not be quite as simple as golf, but they are hardly a mystery even to those who content themselves with armchair play. They know when they have a good chance of making a pot and should therefore attempt it, and when they do not and should play a safety shot. With experience they learn positional play, which is obviously the key to the game, and scorn those who simply bang in a pot and hope for the best. They know all about attempting to lay and attempting to escape from snookers. Every so often they rattle in a difficult long pot not a fluke that would almost force a smile from Jimmy White. And yet they cannot make those elusive big breaks, which alone would demonstrate real improvement. The twenty breaks do not become forty breaks, let alone centuries. In time they become resigned to the fact that they have reached their natural playing level.

The stance

The reason the stance is so important is that at the moment of playing the shot the body should be absolutely still, with the exception of the right forearm. To be still you must be steady as a rock, and there is only one stance that will provide that steadiness, shot in and shot out. The right *leg* should be roughly in line with the shot, with the right *foot* pointing to the right of that line at an angle of about sixty degrees. The left *foot* should be pointing roughly in line with the shot, and the distance between the feet should be twelve inches. The left leg should be bent at the knee, which means the weight is forward, while the right leg must be ramrod straight. This is crucial. The right leg is your anchor and on no account should you move it. Take care that you do not involuntarily rise on your toes while you are making the shot. This is a common fault, easy to spot in other players and easy to cure by concentrating on it until keeping the leg still becomes automatic.

You should find this position both comfortable and solid. If it is not comfortable, a minor adjustment of the feet will make it so. Stick your bottom out as far as it will go. This will make your back level rather than hunched. Guard against having your right leg too far back, as this will make your stance overextended. You may suspect that you make minor variations to this stance from one shot to another, but this is not a worry as long as it remains essentially the same. As to solidity, that is easily demonstrated by adopting the stance and having someone give you a moderate push on the shoulder. You will scarcely move. Then adopt any other conceivable stance and ask for a similar push. The difference will be apparent.

To reach difficult shots without using the rest it is sometimes impossible to adopt the basic stance. This is the exception that proves the rule. Go to any reasonable lengths to avoid using the rest, but beware of overreaching. It is not enough for the cue tip just to be able to reach the cue ball. You must be able to make your preliminary addresses in a straight line, and also be able to follow through.

The grip

The grip is easy. Pick up the cue a few inches from the butt end as if you were going to use it as a club. Relax the tension in your hand. The cue should rest lightly, held just firmly enough to stop it sliding around. You will find that you are holding the cue with the thumb and first two fingers, while it is just resting on the back two fingers. The grip is so natural that there is only one common fault gripping too tightly. This cuts down on the freedom of the cue arm, and it also prevents the natural slight squeeze of the fingers as you strike the ball. This little squeeze is automatic if the cue is held lightly to begin with, and it increases the 'feeling' of the shot.

The bridge

The bridge is important because it is one of the two contacts you have with the cue. And with the feet it forms a tripod, bolting you to the table. Lower your left hand on to the table and spread your fingers as wide as they will comfortably go. Grip the cloth with the finger pads, which will draw the fingers in slightly. Keep the fingers taut and unbent, and draw the thumb in tight to the forefinger. Cock the thumb as far as it will go, forming a V-shaped channel for the cue.

The first time you try to form a bridge it will probably be wobbly and uncomfortable. There will be a tendency to keep the fingers together rather than widely spread, and a temptation to let the thumb wander out, thereby forming the channel between thumb and forefinger rather than on them. Persevere until you get it right. Remember, the wider the base of the bridge, the more solid it will be. And keep the heel of your hand on the table the more contact you have with the cloth the better.

The bridge arm

The great Joe Davis, who virtually invented precision snooker as we know it today, has never been equalled as a theoretician of the game. His penetrating insights were the result of the most rigorous analysis of his own playing technique—not a bad model, since it was good enough to win him twenty consecutive world championships before he retired in 1947. Today's stars agree with virtually everything Davis ever said or wrote about the game—even when they neglect to put it into practice. On one point, though, most tend to disagree, however deferentially.

Extending the left arm

Davis was adamant that the left arm should be thrust out dead straight from the shoulder, to its maximum extension. In theory this makes sense, given the similarity between the action of sighting and cueing a ball and drawing a bow. In Davis's case, the theory and practice dovetailed nicely: he was a relatively small man and with his arm straight out he was at the optimum distance from the cue ball. Much taller players find that pushing the arm straight out leaves them a little too far from the cue ball. This not only f eels awkward but it makes it virtually impossible to follow through properly. The cue should be accelerating to the maximum speed required for the particular shot as it goes *through* the cue ball. You do not want the cue power to be spent by the time the cue actually reaches the cue ball. Tall players find it more comfortable to be slightly more compact on the table, and so they bend the left arm slightly. Steve Davis, who is well over six feet tall, does this to a noticeable extent. Do whichever suits you, bearing in mind that feeling comfortable on the table is a vital consideration and that the whole of the forearm must rest securely on the table.

The cue arm

The emphasis on stance, bridge and bridge arm is in a sense only the means to an end. The end is the cue action itself. Get the cue action right, consistently right, and you are on your way to playing good snooker. In describing the correct cue action, Joe Davis likened it to the movement of a piston. The cue is the piston, the wrist and forearm the connecting rods. This mechanical image is particularly appropriate because it is easily grasped, and it draws attention to the fact that as far as humanly possible the cue action should be mechanical. Like a well-oiled machine, the cue arm should perform the same motion over and over again without any variation.

Adopt the correct stance and form the bridge. Slot the cue into the 'V' of the bridge and lean forward until the cue just brushes your chin beneath your nose. If you are holding the cue a few inches from the butt end, this should bring your right forearm into a vertical position. Consider the elbow as a hinge, from which the forearm will swing easily back and forth, like a pendulum. The vertical position of the forearm at rest is important because it means that the sequence of backswing, strike and follow-through can be accomplished while keeping the cue almost completely horizontal. That is the goal, a horizontal cue action. If the forearm at rest is behind vertical, the cue will tend to come through with a scooping action. If the forearm at rest is in front of vertical, the cue will tend to lift off the bridge on the shot and follow through.

Ideally, there should be a straight line running from the raised right elbow to the tip of the cue. That is the perfect alignment: arm, cue and line of shot as one. Some players fall into it naturally. John Spencer used invariably to be cited as having perfect alignment. In still-life line-up he still does, but his slide down the rankings in recent years is attributable ultimately to the fact that he has lost his straightness of cue action in motion. Television has often shown him not bringing the cue back in a straight line, so obviously he is not bringing it through straight. Steve Davis, on the other hand, was always pretty straight, but he has kept working at it over the years, trying to make and keep it straighter still. With a single exception, all the top players demonstrate nearly true alignment. The exception is sixtimes world champion Ray Reardon. His right elbow juts out alarmingly, which means that his wrist is turned outward as well. This is because Reardon broke his shoulder as a child, and he cannot cue any other way. He insists that the eccentric cue action forced upon him by necessity has never impaired his game, and, with a record like his, who is to argue? All it really proves, however, is that great talent and application can compensate for technical frailty. You will play better snooker if you model your cue action on John Spencer's rather than Ray Reardon's.

Having said that, beware of trying to imitate the television stars in a slavish manner. By all means watch them critically, Try to recognize the strengths and weaknesses in their techniques, and, where you can, apply your observations to your own technique. However, remember that you are an individual, as each of them is, and just as their styles vary one from the other, so must yours be individual. It is the general principles of sound technique that you must acquire, not a copycat image of your favourite player.

Lining up the shot

As well as the piston analogy, Joe Davis likened the cue action to that of a rifle. The V of the bridge is the sight, and what you are trying to do is line up the target along the cue and through that sight. Having done that, you effectively push the cue through the bridge along the sight line. Again, it is an apt image, and it explains why there is so much emphasis placed on complete stillness during the shot. Nothing must move except the trigger finger when you fire a rifle. Nothing must move except the right forearm when you play a shot. It also explains why the head must be right down on the cue, the eyes looking directly along the line of shot.

Here again there are exceptions. If your eyes are of roughly equal strength ' it will be natural to use both of them in sighting the shot. The cue will be brushing the centre of your chin. But if one eye is significantly stronger than the other, you will necessarily favour that eye. Joe Davis had a weak right eye, and he played with the cue running directly beneath his left eye. So does Rex Williams. In a less pronounced way, many players slightly favour one eye, either by a fractional tilt of the head or a minor adjustment of the stance. The most extreme example of all is provided by Graham Miles; not only is he left-eyed, but he has an imposing chin. How do you get right down on the ball when you have such a chin getting in the way? Well, Miles has developed a method of sighting that nearly defies belief. The cue runs beneath his left ear and brushes his left cheek. If he moved it any further out he would be playing on the next table! Try that yourself and you may wonder how Miles can even hit the cue ball, let alone play snooker of the quality that brought him two Pot Black championships in the early 1970s. It is another example of the triumph of talent over technique.

The cueing action

Assume that you have surveyed the table, selected your shot and determined the potting angle. You are perfectly clear in your mind about your intentions. Get into cueing position in line with the shot, with the bridge formed some nine to twelve inches from the cue ball, as feels right. When you are comfortable and confident that you are in the correct position, start addressing the cue ball as a golfer does a golf ball, with several approaches. The purpose of this feathering is threefold. It allows you to check that you are cueing straight and it builds rhythm and it assists concentration, Ignore the example of Jimmy White. First-time sighting and the minimum of preparation work for him, but then when White is in full flood he makes every aspect of the game look ridiculously easy. You know better.

At the same time, there is no point in overdoing these preliminaries, as some players do on even the simplest of pots. Here again the rifle analogy is useful. Just as the marksman is not likely to make his best shot by taking one quick glance down the sight and firing, he is also not going to make it by staring interminably down the sight while trying to hold his body motionless. The longer he waits, the greater the chance of involuntary movement.

Finally, while you are feathering keep your body and head absolutely still. There is nothing whatever to be said for the way Alex Higgins bobs around while he is addressing the ball, all those jerky, twitchy mannerisms, the staccato feathering, that whole collection of eccentricities so hilariously parodied by John Virgo. Higgins is prodigiously gifted, and there may never be anyone to match him when it comes to conveying the sheer thrill of watching genius on the loose. But his style is not for the coaching manual.

Ignore the pocket

While feathering, you should keep checking that your cueing is straight, and that the cue is directed at the point on the cue ball that you want to hit. Meanwhile, your eves will be flickering back and forth between cue ball and object ball, or, rather, between cue ball and the part of the object ball you intend to hit. Remember, you have determined the angle you need on the object ball before getting down over the shot, so you have nothing whatever to think about except hitting the object ball at the point needed to achieve that angle. The pocket by this stage is irrelevant, and you should resist the temptation to look at it. What good is looking at it anyway? It has hardly moved since you selected the angle. If you have got the angle right, and play the shot as you intend, you will make the pot. If you have got the angle wrong you will miss it. If while you are cueing a doubt creeps into your mind about the angle, you must stop. Stop completely that is, not simply change the line of the shot while remaining in the cueing position. Stand up, look at the balls for as long as you need to judge the angle again, and then repeat the cueing sequence. The point is, however, that once you are down on the shot the pocket is a useless distraction. You have as much as you can handle in making sure that you strike the cue ball where you want to strike it, and that in doing so you send it in a straight line to the part of the object ball at which you are aiming.

When you sense that the moment has come to play the shot, you will begin the final backswing. It should be a somewhat shorter backswing than you have been using while feathering, where you were building LIP your rhythm. The rhythm is now there, and when you come to strike the cue ball you want no more backswing than is necessary to make a clean, flowing stroke of the strength required. An exaggerated backswing means that the cue will travel further than it needs to, and the further it travels the more likely it is to go off line. The further it travels the harder it is to keep the cue on the horizontal. Both opinion and practice vary on the extent of the backswing, but for a shot of normal strength five or six inches should be about right.

As you begin that final backswing your eyes should be on the cue ball, checking for the last time that you are going to strike it where you intend. As the backswing progresses at an unhurried pace your eyes should travel from the cue ball to the object ball. And there they should stay, throughout the shot. Your cue arm, cue and eyes are all now together on the line of the shot, and by fixing your eyes on the end of that line you pretty well guarantee that the cue will come through on that line. The cue automatically follows the eye if you are cueing straight.

As you complete that final backswing, eyes now fixed unwaveringly on the object ball, pause for the briefest of moments. Do not overdo it little more than a hesitation. Precisely why this pause is important is not completely clear. Presumably it gives you a final fraction of a second to secure your sight on the object ball, and perhaps it provides a sort of freeze-frame on the whole of the body, bringing everything into unison for the moment of striking. Top golfers provide an analogy. The most fluent swings bring the club smoothly back to a slight pause at the top of the backswing before the club comes down and through. Whatever the reason, there is no disputing its importance in the cueing sequence, although here again you will observe marked differences between the top players. Doug Mountjoy scarcely seems to pause at all, whereas Steve Davis almost allows you to draw in Your breath in anticipation.

Striking the cue ball

The slight pause on the final backswing, eyes on the part of the object ball you are aiming to hit, and now strike cleanly through the cue ball. Do not lift your head or shift your gaze. Keep looking at the object ball as the cue ball makes its journey. Keep looking at it as the cue ball collides with it. Keep looking at it, or, rather, at the spot where it was, after it has disappeared in the direction of the pocket. Keep your eyes on that spot until you hear the satisfying clunk as it hits the bottom of the pocket.

That may sound excessive, since once the cue ball is on its way everything is in the lap of the gods. What earthly difference can it make if you watch it approach the object ball, and then watch the object ball on its way to the pocket? After all, you are keenly interested in the course of the shot, so why not gratify your curiosity? This is the reason. In all games that involve striking a ball, from golf to cricket, from tennis to football, the cardinal sin is to take your eye off the ball before striking. There is an almost irresistible urge to do just that, because once you are committed to making the shot, once you are actually in the throes of doing it, your mind leaps forward to the outcome. And as your mind leaps so do your eyes and head. The only way you can guarantee that you do not take your eyes off the ball before striking it is to force yourself to keep them on the ball, or where the ball was, after striking it. Hence the way the golfer struggles against nature to keep his head down throughout the swing.

It is the same with snooker. You must discipline yourself to keep the head steady for a measurable time after you have struck the cue ball. If you do not do that you will be in grave danger of moving your head before you have struck the cue ball. When that happens, and it will almost certainly be at critical moments when you are most keyed up, you will have destroyed the very basis of the cue action. Marvel if you like at the way Higgins seems to break this rule with impunity the head shooting up as he cracks in some fiendishly difficult long pot. But watch Steve Davis, and follow his example.

Follow-through and stop

Up to and including the pause, each element in the cue action can be examined and practised in isolation. But the strike, follow-through and stop cannot. They are inextricably linked in the one movement. Fortunately, the cue action is a natural one in the sense that the follow-through and the stop follow automatically from a clean strike.

A clean strike is not a push, much less a slash, however powerfully the stroke is played. It is not even a swing, although it should be smooth and flowing. It is best described as a punch, and as with a punch the action continues beyond the point of impact. The extent of the follow-through will depend on the strength of the shot and the intended course of the cue ball following it. However, every shot, including screw, requires follow-through.

Hitting the cue ball straight

Everything to this point has been devoted to the sole end of hitting the cue ball in a straight line. Apart from the rare occasion on which you want to swerve the cue ball, hitting the cue ball straight is an essential part of every successful shot. There is an easy way. to check whether you are cueing straight.

On an empty table, play the cue ball from the brown spot, over the blue, pink and black spots, hard enough to bring the cue ball off the top cushion and back down the table. Because there is no object ball to focus on, treat the blue spot as the object ball during the shot. You should have no difficulty in running the cue ball over the spots on the outward journey, but what happens on the way back? If you are cueing dead straight, and not imparting any unintentional side-spin to the cue ball, it will come back near enough over the spots. It is a foolproof test, and many professional players start every serious practice session with it. When you can do it consistently with a medium strength shot, gradually increase the pace. It gets more difficult as the pace increases, and with a full power shot you will never consistently be closer than a couple of inches from the brown spot on the return. The moral of this is that you should never hit the cue ball harder than necessary to achieve a desired result. The harder you strike it the greater the risk of inaccurate cueing.

Cue ball control

The art of potting

Once you can strike the cue ball in a straight line you are ready to tackle potting. Good potting is essential, for the obvious reason that it is the only feasible way of putting together enough points to win a frame. That is not to deny the importance of snookering your opponent under the right circumstances, but points gained by laying successful snookers can hardly build a winning score. You can only build this by amassing breaks.

Break-building is a combination of accurate potting and sound positional play. Miss the pot, however, and the effort to secure good position for the following shot is wasted. In fact it can easily rebound against you Suppose you are attempting to pot a colour and secure position on the only available red. If you miss the pot but succeed in gaining position on the red your opponent will be very pleased. In such a situation, and it is a common one, getting your shot half right is worse than fluffing it altogether.

It is often said that potting ability is largely innate, that a good potter has 'a good eye, a natural ability to size up angles in a word, flair. Consequently, mediocre potters become resigned to their limitations in this respect. They sigh wistfully as they watch the good potter, the 'born' potter, and reflect on the unfairness of life. They pin their hopes on safety play, but in their hearts they know that the better potter almost always wins, and deservedly so. They are beaten before they begin.

This is largely bunk. Of course it is true that Jimmy White is a born potter, in the sense that he is uncannily gifted at this aspect of the game. However, you are unlikely to be competing against Jimmy White. Good potting is an acquired skill, even for White. You do not need 'a good eye' as you do for games with a moving ball, where you have to be able to gauge speed and flight quickly and accurately almost instinctively. Snooker is a static game, like golf and bowls. As such, it is almost completely dependent upon technique. That is why so much emphasis is placed on cue action. Anyone who pots consistently well has a good cue action. Whether that good cue action was acquired by happy accident, or by diligent practice, is immaterial it is there, on open display. Conversely, no matter how frustratingly inept your potting may be at the moment, if you acquire a good cue action your potting must improve. As it improves, it will make sense for you to turn your attention to the more interesting and rewarding aspects of the game.

Plain ball potting

A plain ball shot is one in which you strike the cue ball dead centre. It is in contrast to spin shots of all descriptions stun, screw, topspin, side, or side in conjunction with one of the others. Novices can hardly wait to attempt these advanced shots, particularly so in these days of televised snooker. The commentators scatter the terms around like confetti, making it pretty apparent that stun, screw and the rest play an enormous part in the game. They do indeed, but there is a snag. When the commentator coolly informs you that Cliff Thorburn is going to play a simple stun on the red, which will bring him nicely on to the black, he neglects to point out a banal truth. Thorburn could not possibly pot the red using stun unless he could pot it with a plain ball shot. He is using stun to gain position for the next shot not because he has a fondness for stun. It follows from this that until you come to terms with plain ball potting you are wasting your time even thinking about the mysteries of spin.

Consider first the matter of potting in a straight line, since this avoids the problem of choosing the correct angle. If the cue ball and object ball are in a direct line with the pocket, it is simply a matter of striking the object ball full face. This shot cruelly exposes flaws in basic technique, and is therefore the natural place to start.

Take the diagonal line between corner pockets and place the cue ball on the baulk line where the diagonal crosses it. Place the object ball a foot the table also on the diagonal. You now have a straight pot into the corner pocket. In theory, you should be able to make the pot consistently. In practice, you cannot consistently. Why? The possible reasons for failure are severely limited. Either you sighted wrongly or struck the cue ball wrongly. If the latter, you must either have lined yourself up incorrectly for the shot or failed to deliver the cue in a straight line. As usual, you have been let down by your technique.

The more grooved your cue action becomes, the more you will succeed with straight pots, especially over distance, which magnifies the effect of any inaccuracy. Straight pots, more than any others, highlight the difficulty posed by distance. With the blue on its spot and the cue ball a few inches away, in direct line with the middle pockets, you have a pot well within reach of the complete novice. With the cue ball in the baulk area and the object ball three-quarters of the way up table, in direct line with a corner pocket, you have a pot that even a world champion would regard as no certainty.

Potting at an angle

The angled potting attempt is far and away the most common shot in snooker. Skill or lack of it in this department is generally decisive in the outcome of any contest. Therefore, any real improvement here is bound to be reflected in your results. What is the secret of potting at an angle?

There is no secret. Indeed such theories as there are on the subject are more of a hindrance than a help. There is a widespread assumption that when snooker balls collide, they are deflected along lines that are predictable by the laws of geometry and basic physics. The idea that snooker is in this sense purely geometrical is a fallacy, but an understandable one. The route taken by the balls following collision is indeed roughly in line with geometry. But it is not exactly geometrical, which means that if you search for the geometrical potting angle you will miss the true potting angle.

The difference between the two angles is easier to demonstrate than it is to explain. The geometrical angle would be achieved by striking the object ball at a point diametrically opposite the pocket. In other words, if at the point of contact between the cue ball and the object ball the two are lined up for the pocket, according to the geometrical principle the object ball should go to the pocket. It should behave as it would have behaved had you played a dead straight pot from directly behind the object ball, because you are striking it at exactly the same point. In practice, if the object ball is within twelve inches or so of the pocket, the geometrical angle will see you home. At double that distance, where the margin of error is less, it will invariably let you down. At eight feet it will lead you astray to an embarrassing degree. The shot will be too thick, because the actual angle of deflection will be less than geometry would have it. The difference between the geometrical and true potting angle is small, but then the difference between making and barely missing a pot is a small one. It is the consequences that loom large.

An explanation of this demonstrable fact must come down to the resistance, or friction, between the balls and the cloth. But the explanation is unimportant. You must accept that for all shots other than straight or nearly straight ones, the geometrical angle is only a near guide to the true potting angle. You must find the true potting angle by experiment, and then commit it to memory.

Potting from memory

Potting angles are chiefly a matter of memory. When good potters say that they know potting angles instinctively, what they really mean is that any potting situation looks familiar to them, and they know from memory how to pot from that particular angle. This may sound implausible, since between a dead straight contact and the finest of cuts there must be an infinite number of possible angles. With the balls spread haphazardly around the table, never the same from one game to the next, how can memory tell you the precise potting angle? Mercifully, snooker has been designed for mortals. Potting may strike you as fiendishly difficult, but it need not be truly precise. A snooker ball is two-and-ones sixteenth inches in diameter. The pocket is three-and-a-half inches across at the fall of the slate, which means that it is a little over one-and-a-half widths of the ball. This provides a decent margin of error to work within, and it means that you need not worry about an infinite number of potting angles.

In practice, potting angles are reassuringly few. There is full ball, which is no angle at all, and there is fine cut, which is as close to ninety degrees as you can manage. Between these extremes are three distinct potting angles: three-quarter ball, half-ball, and quarter-ball.

For the three-quarter ball angle an imaginary line through the centre of the cue ball would run midway between the centre and the outside edge of the object ball. For the half-ball angle, this imaginary line would barely brush the outside edge of the object ball. For the quarter-ball angle it would miss the edge of the object ball by one-quarter its width.

These five angles, from full ball to fine cut, are all you have to burden yourself with. Admittedly, you will find yourself making slight modifications to them as experience dictate. A half-ball angle may be a shade more than half-ball or a shade less, but it is still basically a half-ball angle. If you can recognize it as such, you are on your way to potting it. The really critical judgment is to identify the basic potting angle from any position on the table. A half-ball angle is a half-ball angle wherever it crops up. This means that you should be able to overcome irrational fears about particular potting situations. If you see it correctly as a half-ball pot, and play it that way, you will make the pot whether it is from left to right, right to left, into a middle pocket, into a corner pocket, off the black spot or from the 'D'.

It follows from this that there is no short cut, no magic formula for consistent potting which must be your goal. You must learn to recognize potting angles by trial and error, both in practice and during play. If you persistently miss a particular type of shot, stick with it until you find the right angle. Once you have found it, commit it to memory. And so on to the next. It is a matter of conscious application, of carefully noting what happens when you miss a pot and gaining from the experience, rather than just writing it off.

Learning the angles

Any systematic potting practice is good for locating and memorizing potting angles. Here is one that is not only helpful generally, but specifically geared to improving your score in the next frame you play.

Potting the black is your most eagerly awaited opportunity. To the beginner, and not just the beginner, a black ball pot seems more daunting than an identical red ball pot because the stakes are in pure scoring terms seven times as high. To cure this costly inhibition, practise potting the black off its spot. As the level at which you play snooker improves, potting the black off its spot becomes an increasingly important shot. In the professional game it is the dominant shot because of its pivotal role in most break-building. Therefore the sooner you get used to potting it routinely the better.

Spot the black and place the cue ball so as to leave yourself a quarter-ball pot. Then move the cue ball to the half-ball angle, then the three-quarter, the full, then on to the other three-quarter ball angle, the half, and the quarter. Practise these shots until you feel confident that the angles are locked permanently in your memory. You may never feel confident of making these shots with the clinical ease that the professionals demonstrate, but you will recognize them for what they are. Knowing how to make a particular pot is not the same thing as making it, but it more than somewhat increases your chances.

The world of spin

The plain ball shot is fine for potting, but severely limited for positional play. The reason it is so limited is that the cue ball will be deflected off the object ball on the precise angle predetermined by the potting angle. Since you have no choice about the potting angle, you have no control over the cue ball's leaving angle. It will go where it will go. At least it will do so in terms of direction. You can control the strength, or weight of the shot, and that will determine the distance along the line of direction that the cue ball will travel. However, it is notoriously difficult to control the cue ball with sufficient accuracy using weight alone. Even if you could do so, you would still find your choice of position dictated by that invariable line of departure. With every shot you would be on tramlines for the next.

Spin spells success

Only by breaking free of those tramlines does serious break-building become a realistic possibility. The best potter in the world would be lucky to make a break of forty using plain ball shots alone, and that only under rarely favourable circumstances. He would feel himself in chains. Spin is the great liberator. What spin does—any kind of spin—is alter the course of the cue ball following its collision with the object ball. Topspin and backspin do so immediately. Side-spin takes effect when the cue ball hits a cushion. Side can be used in conjunction with either topspin or backspin.

Topspin

If you strike the cue ball above centre you impart topspin. The higher you strike it the greater the topspin, always providing that the cue tip follows through nicely to accentuate the spinning action. The effect of topspin is to assist the ball's forward motion, so that when it strikes the object ball it runs through further than it would do with a plain ball shot. You have probably hit the odd shot with accidental topspin and with spectacularly awful consequences. You have slammed in an easy straight pot, because slamming it in feels so good, and then watched in horror as the cue ball leapt in pursuit of the object ball, to be happily reunited in the bottom of the pocket. That was topspin, caused in this case by one or more of the familiar deadly sins jerking the head or coming through with a scooping action. Topspin used deliberately, often in conjunction with side, is a valuable addition to your repertoire of shots. When using it, raise your bridge slightly so as to keep the cue action horizontal. Beware of aiming too high on the cue ball it is easy to miscue. The tip of the cue should be travelling at its fastest as it strikes and goes through the cue ball. This is how maximum power and control can be obtained without strain.

Backspin

The repertoire of backspin strokes screw, stun and

drag lie at the heart of snooker. If you strike the cue ball below centre you impart backspin. The lower you strike it the greater the backspin, provided that you follow through correctly. Backspin works against the ball's natural forward motion. The ball is travelling forward, towards the object ball, but it itself is spinning backwards all the time. Upon impact, the backspin counteracts the cue ball's natural forward momentum. The actual effect this has on the cue ball depends upon a combination of factors, and it is the effect that gives rise to the description of the shot as a screw shot, a deep screw shot, a stun shot and so forth.

The language of backspin

It is important to understand the language of backspin here and now, because for the remainder of this book the various terms will be used without further explanation. It is common even for good players to get into a muddle when describing variations of backspin, and if you are confused by the words you will most surely be misled by the information. The difficulty is caused by the use of the word screw in two distinct senses. On the one hand there is screw as in applying screw to the cue ball, or screwing the cue ball. In that sense, screw is used to describe the technique of applying any degree of backspin, whatever the outcome. To play most stun shots or a drag shot you employ screw. The exception to this is where the cue ball and object ball are very close together, when stun will be achieved by central striking or even slightly above centre. Typical stun shots and drag shots are simply two results of employing screw. On the other hand, there is the screw shot itself. The screw shot, like the stun and drag shots, is the particular result of the application of screw. More or less screw, in combination with other factors, will result in a screw shot, a stun shot or a drag shot.

The other factors in the equation are the distance between the cue ball and the object ball and the speed of the cue ball. However much or little screw you apply to the cue ball, the backspin is at its maximum as the ball leaves the tip of the cue. It wears off continuously as the cue ball travels to the object ball. Therefore, the further the cue ball has to travel, and the longer it takes to get there, the smaller the proportion of the original backspin still active upon contact. In consequence, a given amount of screw played over a short distance will have a much greater screwing effect than it will played over a long distance. So will a given amount of screw played with pace rather than gently. Hence, the amount of screw that it takes to stop the cue ball dead upon impact when hit full on to the object ball where the two balls are six feet apart, would bring the cue ball back towards you if the balls were two feet apart.

For the moment, ignore the factors of distance and speed, and ignore to a the distinction between stun and screw. Whichever result you want, you must develop the skill of screwing the ball.

Screwing the ball

For a novice, any shot employing screw is far more difficult than the equivalent plain ball shot. It is not unlikely that you have seen it played consistently well only on television. But if you master it, it will give you a huge, probably decisive, advantage over your opponents until you leave your fellow novices far behind.

Why is it difficult? Because it demands everything the plain ball shot does and a lot more besides. As with the plain ball shot you must determine the correct potting angle and succeed with the pot. At the same time, you must determine the correct striking point on the cue ball and the correct strength of shot to achieve the desired amount of backspin. Following through feels less natural than it does on a plain ball shot. You must be able to work backwards from the desired result to the means of achieving that result. This clearly requires good judgment, based on experience. If, for example, you intended to screw the cue ball back two feet and only screwed it back two inches, you may be in all sorts of trouble.

Lower the bridge

It should be apparent, but it seems not to be, that the application of screw requires an alteration to the bridge. If you aim to strike the cue ball below centre with the normal bridge you will be striking down on it. That means you will be raising your cue arm, dramatically so if you are attempting maximum screw. Naturally this ruins the horizontal cue action. You come through with a scoop, and because burying the tip of the cue in the cloth is the snooker player's worst nightmare, you slam on the brakes the instant you hit the ball. So much for follow-through. And so much for backspin, because you cannot get backspin without following through. What you have is a downward stab, not a screw. The chances are that you will miss the pot, unless it is a sitter, and, to add insult to injury, the cue ball will refuse to screw back so much as an inch.

The horizontal cue action and follow-through can only be achieved by lowering the bridge. The extent to which you lower it is determined by your point of aim on the cue ball. The best way to lower the bridge is to turn the bridge hand inwards, as if you were turning it on to its side. This automatically lowers the thumb and the cue channel. Much of the pressure comes off the little finger, but the bridge should still be solid, with most of the weight on the pad at the base of the thumb. You are now able to strike the cue ball below centre with the horizontal cue action.

With the fear of damaging the cloth removed, it will feel natural to follow through, perhaps not quite so far as with a plain ball shot, but enough to 'feel' the cue ball on the tip of your cue. The slight sensation of 'gripping', as the cue tip bites into the curved surface of the ball, tells you that you have applied screw. It is vital that the cue tip be rounded and well chalked. It is because the professionals use a certain amount of screw in the vast majority of shots that they are in the habit of chalking before every shot.

Players who fail in their attempts with screw usually do so because they strike the cue ball higher than they think they are striking it. They address the ball as though they are going to come through well below centre, but at the last moment they subconsciously raise the line. Fear of an embarrassing miscue, combined with an attempt to use excessive power, is almost invariably the cause. Aim to strike low and *strike low,* which you can do confidently with a horizontal cue. You do not need any extra power to gain screw, although with practice you will find it progressively easier to increase power for greater effect.

Controlled screw

Place a ball on the blue spot with the cue ball about nine inches away, directly in line with a middle pocket. Using normal strength, keep potting the ball using screw. With a little bit of screw the cue ball will stop dead upon impact, With more it will come back, further and further the more screw you apply. As your technique improves and your confidence grows, you should be able to screw the cue ball all the way back to the other side pocket. As with potting angles, you must begin to build a memory bank, so that you can associate a particular amount of screw over a certain distance with a predictable result. Good players Gan screw almost to the inch. When you think you have a pretty fair idea of screwing from nine inches, separate the balls a bit more. And so on. You are now embarked on advanced snooker technique, and it will be apparent to you at once that as your knowledge of screw increases, so the horizons of your game recede. You will soon find that a simple pot with screw is no more difficult than the same simple pot plain ball. On less simple pots, you will find plenty of problems arising from the division of concentration between potting and positions but that is one of the great challenges of the game at any level.

Stun and screw shots

Stun and screw shots, often with the addition of side, form the overwhelming majority in the top-class game. It would be impossible to run up big breaks without them, because they provide the only means of cruising around the black spot for that remorseless red-black, red-black sequence. That is why you hear the words stun and screw continually during a televised match.

Where a screw shot results in the cue ball recoiling upon impact, a stun shot stops it dead in its tracks. This can be useful, not least because for once you know exactly where the cue ball will be for the next shot. The principle of the stun shot is that the backspin, which is wearing off in the course of the cue ball's journey, must have just enough life left in it at the moment of impact to check the ball's normal forward momentum. The closer the balls are together, the less the backspin required. Too much screw and you have a screw shot, too little and you have stun run-through. Experience must be your guide.

Stun run-through

Stun run-through is a handy variation. Suppose on a straight pot you want to run the cue ball through just a few inches less than it would run through with a plain ball shot struck normal weight. You could try a very slow plain ball shot, but that is ill-advised because really slow shots expose you to the vagaries of the table or the slightest tremour in your cue arm. Stun run through is the answer. Strike the cue ball a little higher than you would for that particular stun shot, but still below centre. With normal weight, the cue ball will follow through, but not as far as it would with a plain ball shot.

Full ball shots provide unambiguous evidence of the application and limitations of screw, because there is no deflection to complicate the equation. A good player should have no difficulty in screwing back eight or ten feet from a distance of two feet. Assuming you have control, that opens up an enormous range of positional opportunities. At a distance of eight feet, you would need pretty well maximum screw and maximum power to stun the cue ball. You will have seen the professionals screw back half the table from a distance of eight feet, but that is a truly prodigious feat. Combining that much power with perfect timing and accuracy is given only to the Jimmy Whites of this world. If you can screw back a foot or so at six feet and stun at eight, you are doing well.

Useful as screw is for gaining position off a straight pot, it is with angled pots that it really comes into its own. It widens the angle at which the cue ball comes off the object ball. The more screw you apply, the wider the angle. This takes you well and truly off the tramlines. In particular, that congested area around the black spot begins to open up for you. It may be heavy traffic, but you are no longer careering about out of control. You can go where you want, within the limitations imposed by your mastery of screw. Just as important, you can avoid going where you least want to go, which is in-off. The unavoidable in-off is one of the great hazards of the plain ball shot. Screw makes the unavoidable avoidable.

Using drag

The drag shot has only one application, but it is a common one. When you want to send the cue ball a long way down the table and leave it there, how can you go about it. How can you play a soft shot at a great distance? You could trickle the cue ball the length of the table, but experience will have taught you how dangerous that is. Even if your aim is perfect, the table almost certainly is not, and a really slow shot over a long distance is likely to go critically off line. The answer is drag. If you strike really low with normal strength, imparting plenty of backspin, the cue ball will make most of its journey at speed, only to slow down at the end as the backspin takes its toll. The effect is that of playing a slow shot at much closer range.

Two common situations demand drag. If you have a long pot on a red at the top of the table, drag enables you to stay up there for the black. If to play safe you have to send the cue ball from the top of the table deep into baulk, hit the object ball so as to bring it off the baulk cushion and back up the tab meanwhile leaving the cue ball near the baulk cushion, drag is your shot.

Applying side

Side adds quite fiendish complications to the shot without corresponding benefits unless and until you understand its workings well and possess good enough technique to employ it properly. The average player frequently misses his pots or messes up his position either because he has inadvertently applied side, or deliberately applied it without a clear understanding of its effects. There should at this stage be no need to labour the point that if you do not know where the cue ball is going to go without side, you are hardly going to be able to gauge the effect of side.

What side does

The principal effect of side is to alter the normal angle at which the cue ball comes off the cushion after contact with the object ball. If the cue ball strikes the cushion dead on at a ninety degree angle without side, it will rebound directly back along the line of approach. If it strikes the cushion at that angle with right-hand side it will come off at an angle to the right; with left-hand side to the left. It follows that if it strikes the cushion coming from left to right, right-hand side will widen the angle of departure, left-hand side will narrow it. Coming on to the cushion from right to left, right-hand left-hand side will have the opposite effect. Playing the cue ball off the cushions from different angles with right-hand left-hand side will quickly show you the extent to which side does this.

You apply side by striking the cue ball to the right or left of centre. It is imperative, however, that you strike straight through the cue ball, which means that the line of the shot must be through the point on the cue ball at which you are aiming. You court certain disaster if you get down over a shot as though to play plain ball, decide that you want to use side and simply redirect your cue tip. By striking across the ball you will most certainly swerve it off line if, that is, you avoid miscueing. The principle is the same as it is over second thoughts about potting angles. You must get up from the shot, adjust your stance slightly in line with your revised intentions, and reposition your bridge so that you are in line with the right or left side of the cue ball.

As with screw, there are two reasons why you might fail to achieve the desired spinning action with side. They are the same two reasons. Either you are not following through or, more likely with side, you are not striking far enough to the side of the cue ball even though you may think you are. A conscious or subconscious fear of miscueing causes you to drift back to the safety of the centre at the moment of delivering the stroke. That last check on the position of the tip in relation to the cue ball during the final backswing is your invaluable guide.

This matter of actually striking the cue ball where you think you are striking it becomes increasingly critical as you move on to the advanced shots. Consider the combination of deep screw with maximum side. This is an advanced shot in anybody's book, but it is frequently the best or only answer to a tricky positional situation, and it is therefore an essential stroke in any serious player's repertoire. You must strike well below centre, and well to the side—and straight, with follow-through... not forgetting to make the pot. You are deliberately accepting very narrow margins for such a shot, and success depends on your striking the cue ball spot on. The better, and therefore more ambitious, a player you become, the more you will realize the difficulty of doing that. Joe Davis was of the opinion that the main reason why he was so good at the game why he was so much better than you, to put it bluntly was that he struck the cue ball where he intended to strike it, and you do not. Davis did not mean to be cruelly dismissive by this assertion, merely to focus attention on the fundamental importance of basic technique.

Once you have got the knack of applying it properly, the complexities of side begin in earnest. The purpose of side is to redirect the cue ball late in the lifetime of the shot after contact with the object ball and a cushion, However, the effects of side operate throughout the shot, right from the beginning, When you apply right-hand side, the cue ball is initially pushed off course lightly to the *left* by the cue thrust, before the anticlockwise spin brings it back to the *right*. Conversely with left-hand side. The cue ball is therefore describing a slight arc throughout its journey.

It may reach the object ball *before* getting back to the true line, or *after* crossing over that line.

A slight change of aim

Obviously there is some particular distance at which the true line is reached at the point of contact, but when using side you will frequently find that you have to alter your normal aim slightly in order to make the pot. This is more a matter of touch than conscious aiming as several factors, such as the condition of the cloth, can have a distinct bearing. And what deviation there is can be minimized by both smooth striking and follow-through.

Speed also affects the equation. The greater the speed, the further the cue ball will travel before the side counteracts the initial thrust in the opposite direction. Say the balls are three feet apart. Played slowly with right-hand side, the cue ball will have recovered from the initial thrust and moved across the line to the right by the time of contact. With normal pace it should be just about on line. Played hard, it will not quite have got there. The nap of the cloth too affects side. The heavier the nap, the greater the effect of spin. It follows from all these variables that long-distance shots played slowly with side are virtually suicidal, since calculating the drift accurately is beyond the capabilities of even the best players. Only by trial and error and careful observation will you discover your own safe margins for using side. As a rule you should be chary of going much beyond eighteen inches to the object ball. More than three feet is risky for anyone.

So far, the assumption has been that the shot is played up the table, with the nap. If it is played towards baulk, against the nap, it becomes even trickier. This is because running against the nap the spin works in reverse. With right-hand side, there is the usual initial thrust to the left. But instead of the right-hand side then bringing the ball back to the right, it continues to push it out to the left throughout its journey. This makes the slow shot with side utterly treacherous, and the best players discount it out of hand. Yet it is not uncommon to see club players attempting to hit a slow shot the length of the table, against the nap, with maximum side. They should consider themselves fortunate if they even make contact with the object ball.

Assuming you can apply side correctly, and are prepared to do so within sensible limitations of distance and speed, there remains yet another complication. Side slightly alters the angle at which the object ball is thrown by the cue ball. You must adjust the potting angle accordingly. Take, for example, a half-ball pot up table on a spotted black, with the cue ball to the right of the black. If you strike the black at the half-ball angle for a plain ball shot with right-hand side, the black will go to the left of the pocket too fine. With left-hand side it will miss to the right too thick. At this point you could be forgiven for thinking that side is more trouble than it is worth, but in fact experienced players use side so much that they quite automatically make the necessary adjustments to the potting angles.

The myth of transmitted side

Apart from altering slightly the angle at which it is thrown, side has no discernible effect on the object ball. There is not a shred of evidence to support the widely-held belief that side is transmitted to the object ball. However, while ignoring the myth of transmitted side, it is worth considering the one particular circumstance that its believers always bring up in evidence. That is where you are potting down the cushion.

This is always a difficult shot because you have the minimum of pocket to aim for. According to the myth of transmitted side, running side increases the chances of making the pot. The theory is that the anticlockwise spin on the cue ball is transmitted to the object ball, which is therefore inclined to hug the cushion as it runs along towards the pocket. The truth is that most players do indeed find it easier to make the pot with running side, but transmitted side is not the correct explanation. The way to make the pot, with or without side, is to strike the cushion ever-so fractionally before the object ball, with quite a soft shot. Running side may have two beneficial effects in this instance. First, as the cue ball approaches the cushion and object ball, which it must hit almost simultaneously, it will be curving slightly inwards, so that at the point of impact it is marginally more behind the object ball, in line with the pot. Second, running side widens the angle at which the cue ball comes off the cushion as it strikes the object ball. This effectively keeps the cue ball on the potting line fractionally longer than would otherwise be the case. The combined effect of these two factors should not be exaggerated, but if running side increases your confidence with this shot by all means use it.

The swerve shot

Swerve is an extreme form of side. With side, the cue ball curves to a degree, which generally speaking is a nuisance because it adds an unwanted variable to the shot. Sometimes, however, the curving effect can be turned to advantage. If you are in a position where you can almost but not quite achieve a potting angle, because of an intervening ball, side may do the trick. In the same way, side may be sufficient to get you out of the mildest of snookers. But if you are well and truly blocked by an intervening ball, ordinary side will not get you out of the trouble. A great many snookers demand an escape route off one or more cushions, but by no means all. Swerve can be the answer.

To play a swerve shot you break the rule of horizontal cueing. You strike downward on the cue ball, with side. This exaggerates the initial thrust off line before the side takes effect, thereby curving the cue ball right around the intervening ball to get to the object ball. It is not enough merely to raise the butt in order to get the downward angle. The bridge should be raised as well, with the palm coming right off the table. Avoid the common error of striking high on the cue ball. Strike it below centre to maximize the swerve. And break the rule about following through. There should be almost no follow-through with a swerve shot.

This shot requires considerable practice, in order to discover the combination of downward angle, amount of side and strength of shot to achieve any particular line of swerve. Except by accident, it is quite impossible to be absolutely accurate with swerve, and it must therefore be viewed as a purely defensive stroke. You might indeed pot a ball sitting over the pocket with a swerve shot, but then you could pot a real sitter using the wrong end of the cue.

The masse shot

What swerve is to side, masse is to swerve. It is swerve to the ultimate degree. The masse shot plays a far greater role in billiards than it does in snooker, but to be a complete snooker player you must learn it. The masse is called for when a swerve shot would not get the cue ball back from its outward curve in time to make contact with the object ball. This arises where there is only a short distance between cue ball and intervening ball, or between intervening ball and object ball, or both.

The exotic sounding masse shot looks extraordinary because it is at complete variance with every other shot in the game. The cue is struck downwards, practically from the vertical. The cue grip is normal, but a little shorter than usual. The elbow of the bridge arm is wedged against the side of the body for steadiness. The shoulders are as braced as they can be. The bridge hand is completely transformed. Three fingers form a tripod, while the thumb and index finger form a channel of sorts. The wrist is sharply arched, and the palm is facing outwards. It is altogether a weird-looking stroke, but a highly effective one.

Not surprisingly, it requires a great deal of practice to work out the various degrees of spin required to bend the ball to your will. How the cue ball will spin depends upon where you hit it obviously either right or left, as required, but there is more to it than that. If you come down on the front of the upper surface you will get topspin. The ball will initially go slowly backwards, and then leap forwards with a strong combination of topspin and side. If you come down on the back of the ball you will get backspin. The ball will initially go slowly forwards, and then race backwards with extreme side. As with swerve, there should be no follow-through.

The power shot

The true power shot, as opposed to a shot played with considerable pace, is immensely difficult, and most professionals use it sparingly. The problem with it is that it forces you to break the cardinal rules concerning cue action. The longer backswing needed to generate real power, the hard strike and full follow-through conspire to play havoc with that smooth, sweetly-grooved action. There is almost bound to be movement of the shoulder as you feel yourself putting your whole body into the shot, and the head will inevitably rise. You must do what you can to minimize such movement by bracing yourself even more firmly than usual, making an especially firm bridge and so on but movement and therefore less accuracy is the price you pay for a power shot. Follow the example of the professionals, and only attempt a power shot when you have no other means of gaining position. Having said that, observe how a player like Jimmy White, who plays power shots superbly, obtains his power not with a massive swing but by maximum controlled acceleration through the cue ball. Uncontrolled power spells disaster, so resist the temptation to have a bash.

Awkward bridging

Snooker would be a much easier game if it were always possible to form a bridge in the orthodox manner. That it is not so is a problem that confronts the novice right from the start. He finds that his previous shot, or his opponent's, has left the cue ball too near a cushion for the bridge to be formed comfortably if at all. Or he faces the even more intimidating task of cueing over one or more intervening balls. Really awkward bridging is hazardous for even the best players, and they must cope with it continually because leaving the cue ball close to, and preferably tight against, a cushion is the central feature of most safety play. For the novice, and even the player of reasonable skill, awkward bridging can trigger panic. There is a temptation to hurry the shot to get the unpleasant experience over with and this almost certainly is to transform a difficulty into a disaster. The vital rule, therefore, is to approach the situation calmly and deliberately.

Using the various rests

player welcomes a position from which he must use the rest or, worse, the spider or one of the longer cues and rests. Any of these implements necessarily restricts cue control. There is a temptation, therefore, to go almost to any lengths to avoid using them. You will have seen ordinary players both overreaching and accepting a ludicrously large distance between bridge and cue ball. It is also common enough for players to shun the rest and thereby ignore perfectly reasonable potting opportunities. Either of these mistaken practices will hinder your progress. The rest and its fellows must be viewed in the same light as the various supplementary bridges. They are there to help you when you need them. Learn to use them correctly.

7

SPECIAL SHOTS

Doubling the ball

Novices tend to enjoy playing doubles, whereas professionals are chary of them. The reason for this is simple enough. The novice is not really expecting to bring the shot off, and when he not infrequently does it looks and feels a spectacular shot particularly if he has really cracked it in. The professional has no interest in spectacular looking shots. He is invariably looking for ways to make things as easy as possible for himself and cares nothing for flourishes, everything for keeping the break going. Unlike the novice, the professional always expects to make his pots, and for the most part he will prefer not to play a double unless he can do so with small risk and the prospect of significant profit.

There are inherent problems with doubles. One is that it is unsettling to be aiming for a pocket that is completely out of your vision. As you shape up for the shot you have to imagine where the pocket is. For another, you are involved with two angles rather than the single one of a normal pot. You must figure out the angle the object ball must take off the cushion in order to reach the pocket, and then figure out the angle you need on the object ball in order to bounce it off the cushion at that angle. Finally, you have to be aware of the nature of the cushions themselves.

If you play the shot with normal strength, the object ball will rebound at the reverse angle to that at which it arrived. If you bang the ball hard against the cushion, however, it depresses the cushion to such a degree that the angle of departure becomes unpredictably narrower. Doubles should therefore never be played hard. Some like to play them hard not just because of the satisfying effect if they go in, but because they are afraid of leaving the object ball, on' if they miss. That is a complete mistake. If you play the shot with normal strength and fail, at least the object ball will not be sitting over the pocket. Play it as a power shot and it could go anywhere, scattering other balls around in a completely unpredictable way. Scattering balls around the table in a haphazard fashion is something the good player never does.

Having looked at the dark side of the double, especially the foolish banged one, it must be emphasized that the judicious double is a most valuable stroke to learn. Many a big break hinges, at one point or another, on pulling off a double.

Trial and error

As with potting angles, the only way you will learn to make doubles is through trial and error, and by careful observation of what happens when you attempt them from various positions. Sometimes it helps to go to the intended pocket and, imagine the shot backwards.

One marginal advantage the double has over normal shots is that once you have settled on the angle, you can give over your entire concentration to cue ball control. There is no pocket in vision to distract you. You must work on the assumption that the double will succeed, and therefore make certain of position. It is quite maddening to pull off a difficult double and find you have left yourself with nothing 'on'.

You should also note the fact that professionals, wherever possible, play doubles as 'shots to nothing'. By far the most commonly played doubles are into the middle pocket where the cue ball is reasonably close to the opposite side cushion. Doubles can also be played into a corner pocket, but this shot should be regarded with the greatest of care and caution. If you miss it, the object ball has a nasty habit of wobbling about in the jaws of the pocket, to leave your opponent a sitter. Because of this danger, professionals faced with a corner-pocket double always examine the possibility of the 'cocked-hat double'.

The cocked-hat double

This could be properly described as a treble, since it involves playing the object ball off three cushions into a middle pocket. It may strike you as fanciful that you could succeed with such a shot other than by luck, but it is not as difficult as it appears. Unlike the corner pocket, the middle pocket is comparatively open. Moreover, if you miss it, the object ball will run free of the pocket, assuming you have played the shot with reasonable strength. Obviously you should never play any double at pocket weight, since that risks leaving a sitter. The snag with the cocked-hat double is that if you just barely miss it, the object ball can go in unpredictable directions. Miss it cleanly and the object ball will carry on towards the other end of the table and, presumably, safety. However, if it hits the facing angle of the middle pocket it may shoot straight back from where it came; or, it may come out of the jaws of the pocket in the direction of the opposite middle pocket. Do not, however, dwell overly on the risk factor. It is fairly rare in snooker to play a shot that carries no risk, which is something you must simply accept.

Finally, there is the type of double you more frequently see, and play, as a fluke than as a deliberate shot: the double played off one of the end cushions either into a side pocket or a corner pocket at the other end. Because it is assumed to be a fluke it causes merriment, but under some circumstances it is perfectly sensible to combine the possibility of such a double with a safety stroke. If it comes off, consider it a bonus.

Sets and plants

Television commentators have fallen into the habit of describing two slightly different types of shot under the umbrella term 'plant'. Strictly speaking, a plant is a position in which it is possible to play one object ball on to another in such away that the second object ball will be potted. Obviously this can apply only to reds except in free ball situations and it really applies only to positions in which a player would actively consider taking on such a shot. Theoretically, there are plants available whenever there are red balls in the open, maybe dozens of them. Poor players, especially those who indulge themselves in really banging the balls around the table, fluke reds off plants all the time. If the two object balls under consideration are actually touching, the proper term for the position is a 'set'. For the purposes of this description the distinction between the two will be kept, although elsewhere in the book 'plant' will be used to describe both, in keeping with current usage.

Sets

The typical set is a situation in which two reds are directly in line with a pocket. It is often assumed that such a pot is unmissable—that it is, in fact, a gift shot. If ever they miss them, players assume that they were wrong in their original assessment of the situation, that the balls were not in fact in line with the pocket. In this they are more than likely to be wrong. If you take a careful look at touching balls and judge them to be directly in line with a pocket, you are almost certainly right—right within the margins provided by the size of the pocket. How, then, can such a shot go wrong?

It can go wrong with the greatest of ease. Most of the time, you will instinctively play the first red as though the second were not there. You will, in other words, play the first against the second along the true potting line. If you do that, the second red will go straight to the pocket, every time. Sometimes, however, either from carelessness or for positional reasons, you may strike the first red entirely differently. That is when you miss the pot.

The 'squeeze' effect

The term usually applied to this phenomenon is 'squeeze'. The force imparted to the first red by the cue ball, being off the potting line, is said to have the effect of squeezing the second red so that it comes off at a slightly different angle and therefore off the potting line. If the two reds are close to the pocket your error will go unpunished. The further they are from the pocket, and the slower you play the shot, the greater the deviation from the potting line. The conclusion is: when the touching balls are in line with the pocket, you must play as though you were attempting to pot the first, so as to send the second off on the true line.

Having made a mental note to heed this cautionary advice, it may occur to you that it opens up fascinating possibilities. If playing 'wrongly' can destroy a natural set, does it not follow that playing 'wrongly' can create a set where the balls are not quite in line with the pocket? The answer is that it most certainly can. That is why you see the professionals peering so intently at possible sets; they can see at a glance whether the touching balls are directly in line with the pocket. What they are peering at is touching balls off line, but close to it; they are looking to create a set. By a little simple experimentation, you should be able to get a pretty fair idea of the practical limitations, and therefore uses, of this type of shot.

Before you do so, however, you must take aboard one final peculiarity about the off-true set. You would probably assume that it would work the same way as a plant does, that you would strike the first red as You would strike it were the balls a little way apart. To pull the line from right to left, for instance, you would think that you would hit the left-hand side of the first red. In reality, you do the opposite. To pull the line from right to left, you aim for the right-hand side of the first red. The further to the right you aim, the further you pull it —it is one of the mysteries of the universe.

Finally, the circumstances of a set have an effect on screw. If you play a set full ball with screw, you will discover that the screw is accentuated. It is as though you were playing into an object ball of double the weight, which means double the resistance to the forward momentum of the cue ball, which is fighting against the backspin. You must adjust your expectations of screwing distance accordingly.

Plants

If the two object balls are not touching, the set becomes a plant. The easiest plants are those in which the two reds are very close together, and both directly in line with the pocket, like a natural set. The further the reds are apart, and the further they are from the pocket, the more difficult the plant. In either case, the principle for playing this successfully is the same. You must cannon the first red into the second as though the first one were the cue ball and effectively pot the second with the first. This means the shot must be played with a very high degree of accuracy, because the slightest error or misjudgment over the contact angle on the first red will be magnified during the second phase of the shot.

Judging the angle

To judge the angle, you should address the first red as though it were the cue ball, and then try to carry the mental image of the two reds in line with the pocket with you as you return to the cue ball to select your angle. Plants are delightfully satisfying shots to bring off successfully, but initially you should resist the temptation to be very ambitious with them. There is every danger of leaving a ball 'on' if you miss, and where feasible you should consider playing them as shots to nothing'. And do not get so carried away with the fine calculations that you ignore positive position.

You should not be taking on the plant unless you think you will get it, and there is precious little point in getting it if it merely results in your ending the break. As your confidence grows, therefore, take on the less difficult plants willingly and positively.

As an interesting aside, it may have struck you on occasion that the Canadian professionals seem to have a particular fondness for plants, that they seem to be a little more ambitious with them than do the other players. The reason for this is that in Canada, both snooker and pool are widely played, and in their youth Thorburn and the others became expert at the American game. Plants, called combination shots in pool, figure largely in that game because the pockets are much bigger in relation to the balls than they are in snooker, thereby giving a greater margin of error. From this experience, the Canadians habitually see possible plants where their fellow professionals do not. All of them, however, keep a beady eye out for sets and plants, and so should you.

Finally, there is an unconventional kind of plant which is really like a deliberate in-off. It sometimes presents itself when the second object ball, either red or colour, is very close to the pocket, and there is room for the first object ball either to enter the pocket direct or be cannoned into it off the second object ball. Clearly, if the second object ball is not 'on' this can be risky, but if a so-called 'wide' pocket is thus created it is there to be taken advantage of.

Trick shots

Trick shots have nothing to do with snooker proper, but occasional televised displays of them have proved immensely popular. Generally speaking, trick shot routines are featured at the end of exhibition evenings or when a one-sided match has ended long before the anticipated time. All the top players can do them, although the most widely-known and popular routines are those of Dennis Taylor, whocan convulse an audience with his accompanying line in Irish gags, and John Virgo, who so delightfully parodies his fellow players.

Some trick shots are very difficult, but by no means all. The examples described below can be mastered with varying degrees of ease by the average player. They are fun to practise, and of course once you have learned them you will be able to choose your moment to entertain and impress your friends.

The unmissable plant

If you can deliver the cue even halfway straight you will make this shot first time. As near as anything ever is, it can be described as unmissable.

Place the blue on its spot, with a red touching it in direct line with the pink and black spots. Place the cue ball on the brown spot. The three balls are now directly in line up the centre of the table. Your claim is that you can pot the blue in either middle pocket as requested guaranteed.

To bring it off, all you have to do is strike the blue either side of centre, on the side opposite the nominated middle pocket. If you want to pot it in the left middle pocket, you Gan strike it anywhere at all to the right of centre. Similarly, in the other direction. With the balls set up accurately, anything but full ball will result in a potted blue. Plain ball will do nicely.

Black in the middle

This is not unmissable means difficult. Like so many trick shots it is a cunning plant that at first sight looks impossible.

The three reds and the black are all touching, and all firmly on the cushion. The fourth red is a quarter of an inch from the touching group, and a half a ball's width from the cushion. The fifth is a ball's width out from the middle pocket. Play the cue ball medium strength with plenty of screw. The black should go in-off.

Zigzag

This is the most difficult so far described because it is a power shot using side, but it is worth persevering with because the effect is spectacular. Place the eleven reds and black as indicated, and the cue ball near the green spot. Play a power shot with moderate screw and right-hand side, aiming for the cushion where indicated. The idea is to come off the cushion on to the first red, cannon off the red back on to the cushion, then on to the second red, then the cushion and so on down the line, until the cue ball finally pots the black. You will have to experiment in order to find the exact point on the cushion to aim for, and since that point is absolutely critical to setting up the chain reaction you cannot be absolutely certain of bringing off the shot. If you find the shot initially beyond you, reduce the number of reds thereby allowing you to play the shot with less power while you work out the line of shot.

The snake

This plant on the black employs all fifteen reds, and it is as easy to play off as it is exhilarating to view.

Place the balls as indicated, about three inches apart with the final red and the black directly in line with the pocket. This is a power shot, played full on the first red, plain ball. If it goes wrong you have not been sufficiently careful in setting up the snake—probably by making it excessively wriggly, which will result in too thin a contact between the reds at the extremes of the curves.

8

THE INNER GAME

Once your game progresses beyond a rudimentary stage, which should happen quickly if you apply yourself, you will need no telling what your strong and weak points are. You will know well enough that, say, you are getting pretty useful around the black spot, but remain painfully insecure when it comes to long pots out of the baulk area. You will perhaps be able to take pride in the fact that you can screw the cue ball more or less as you intend, but the added complication of side defeats you defeats you in the sense that what you gain in positional terms is offset by a reduction in potting accuracy. You will, for the sake of argument, have fallen quite easily into the various techniques for awkward bridging around the cushions, yet fear the rest like the plague. Most important of all, you will know whether your cue action is dependable, requiring only periodic monitoring, or whether it is erratic, never safely left to its own devices but always needing conscious scrutiny.

As with any skill, to achieve your full potential at snooker you must accept the need to practise. Even if you have no ambitions beyond playing competently with your friends, you will find practice rewarding. If you want to progress much beyond that, you will find it essential. The top professionals vary considerably in the importance they attach to practice as far as their own game is concerned. More accurately, they vary considerably in the amount of practice they find appropriate to their own needs. But of course all the top professionals practise regularly.

Why the pros keep practising

They must do so for two reasons. First, even the best of them strive continually to get even better Steve Davis, for instance, practises like a demon, convinced that there are areas of the game' where he can still improve. The second reason is even more important. They must practise to remain as good as they are. It is through practice that they iron out technical imperfections that keep creeping in to threaten their consistency in matchplay. They cannot afford to shrug their shoulders when they lose form for some reason or other. They must discover the reason and cure the fault.

Realistically, your experience of practice will be different from theirs, even if your approach should be the same. If you have the chance, you should practise as much as you can as a beginner. That way you will avoid getting bogged down at the most rudimentary level of play. The game is a great deal more enjoyable if you play at least to a reasonable standard. However, even if you wanted to, you probably, do not have the opportunity to put in several hours of practice a day, day after day. And even if you did, such a routine might bore you quickly. Be commonsensical about it. What are your ambitions in the game? If they really are to beat Steve Davis, then you will have to approach it with the awesome single-mindedness that he has possessed since youth. If your ambitions are more modest than that, tailor your practice to suit. Suppose you like to play with friends, a few·times a week. Try to set aside perhaps an hour a week for practice, either on your own or with a friend. Then make that practice session really concentrated. Work consciously on those aspects of the game that most trouble you. And vary your practice so as to maintain a high interest level. Never practise the same shot over and over again to the point of tedium. Tie your practice sessions in with your actual play as closely as possible. That is, consciously apply anything you have learned at the first opportunity in a game. Try to incorporate each improvement permanently into your game, and then go back to the practice table to grapple with another difficulty. If you practise in this deliberate fashion, you will find it both enjoyable and rewarding—it is well worth giving over a couple of frames table-time for this.

If your sights are set higher than enjoyable friendly snooker, if, for example, you are determined to make progress in the amateur game at increasingly competitive levels, the same applies. But you will have to practise more as well as play more. In that case you really will have to be ruthless with yourself in analysing your game. Like stripping down a car prior to rebuilding it, you will have to break the game down into its many component parts and work tirelessly at them. There is no other way of assembling a really formidable game, a game that will allow you to hold your own and win against increasingly skilled opposition. There are no short cuts to excellence.

The mental game

There is a world of difference between playing a

friendly game in a club and matchplay, but certain key qualities of mind have a bearing on either situation. There is, in fact, a conspicuously high level of conscious mental activity in snooker. There is nothing instinctive about the game, as there is in any game with a moving ball where reactions figure largely. Every time you approach the table you are faced with a decision, or maybe a set of decisions that are interdependent. Are you going to take on the easy pot from which it is difficult to gain position, or the more difficult pot from which it is easy to gain position? If you take the easy pot and fail to get position, how will you be fixed for making a safety shot? If you take on the more difficult pot and miss it, what will you leave your opponent? At the particular stage of the game at which you find yourself, should you be viewing the situation in an aggressive or defensive light? And so on, almost ad *infinitum.*

Choice of shot is a profoundly important aspect of snooker, and of course it is entirely mental. In a friendly match, with nothing at stake, it may not feel much of a burden. The pressure of matchplay alters that, although in reality the correct choice of shot in a friendly, with all factors properly taken into account, should be the correct choice of shot in other circumstances too. It is the pressure to make the correct choice that is different. Time and again you will have seen the finest players visibly agonizing over choice of shot. No chess player could be weighing more finely the pros and cons of various courses of action. And choose they must, either for better or worse.

Having chosen the shot, you must decide how to play it technically, and then ensure that all the technical aspects of the shot are properly performed to achieve the desired result. At a critical point in a match you will naturally be more concerned about the outcome of the shot than you would be in a friendly, and if that concern becomes apprehension, or even fear, it will be more difficult to execute the shot. You will have seen demonstrations of the killing pressure a player can be under time and again. For the spectator, it is riveting. It can make the shot almost unbearable; for some, it is actually unwatchable. Take two memorable examples. Thorburn's legendary 147 break against Griffiths in the 1983 Embassy World Championship appeared to be moving towards a triumphant conclusion as he potted the final red and prepared himself for the fifteenth consecutive black. With the black safely down, it would simply be a matter of clearing the colours from their spots. Thorburn, like all the top players, can clear spotted colours in his sleep. All he had to do was pot the black and bring the cue ball down the table to get nicely on to the yellow. In the event, he made a bit of a hash of that final black. He potted it of course, but the cue ball fell well short of his intended position. Instead of an easy yellow he faced a rather difficult one.

The mental game

It was not fiendishly difficult, but the cue ball was much too far from the yellow for comfort particularly at such a tense stage. And of course the difficult pot carried a further danger. In making it, there was every chance of finishing awkwardly on the green. One of the cruel features of snooker is that drifting out of position tends to have a cumulative effect. Thorburn groaned as he saw the cue ball pull up short. His shoulders sagged. He grimaced with self-disgust. He looked for all the world as if he would have welcomed the hangman. Then he pulled himself together and made a full-blooded pot, coming perfectly on to the green. Sheffield's Crucible Theatre erupted. Thorburn's sigh of relief was echoed in front of millions of television screens. It was, under the circumstances, one of the finest shots ever played.

Two years later, in that most memorable of finals, Steve Davis and Dennis Taylor played to the ultimate death—a black ball finish in the final frame. After exchanging safety skirmishes, Taylor took on a difficult pot, missed it and left Davis with a fine cut back into the top pocket. Because the cue ball was close to the cushion and the pocket only peripherally in vision it was a more difficult shot than it may have appeared to the millions who had stayed glued to their television sets into the small hours. But it was still not that difficult for a player of class, let alone the incomparable Davis. Taylor slumped in his chair, a beaten man. Davis, quite ashen from strain as well as exhaustion, missed the pot badly, leaving Taylor with an easy pot for victory. The crowd gasped with disbelief. Davis looked as shattered as he felt. Moments later it was all over, in a surge of jubilation around the underdog Taylor, while the stricken Davis was alone with his thoughts. Not only was and is he the most technically accomplished of players, he has earned a reputation for being marvellous under pressure every bit as good as Thorburn, and yet, on this occasion ...

It would be far-fetched to imagine that you will ever shape up for a pot under such a strain as Davis endured on that occasion, but matchplay at any level creates pressures. You may be by nature good at coping with pressure or not so good, in which case you will have to discipline yourself. Even a real bag of nerves can, with effort, overcome the worst excesses of this condition.

Matchplay temperament

The word that most closely describes the ideal mental and emotional state for matchplay is composure. To be composed is not to be relaxed, let alone nonchalant. It is to be calm, calm yet alert. Players of any game who are said to have a great temperament have this ability to remain composed under pressure. They are obviously on their toes, concentrating fiercely, keyed up to a pitch that others might find unbearable. Adrenaline courses through their veins yet they remain in control, mentally and physically.

Most of the great snooker players, although not all, have excellent temperaments for the game. The most illuminating example of temperament, however, is provided by tennis. Bjorn Borg was said to have not just a good, but a perfect temperament. The interesting thing is that it apparently did not come naturally to him. As a promising junior, Borg was prone to fits of temper tantrums, racket-throwing, the whole sorry scene that we have become accustomed to on tennis courts. After one particularly bad outburst, he was given a stern dressing down by his coach and mentor, who warned him that if he did not put a stop to such antics he could kiss his chances of success goodbye. Without self-control, he would never be a champion. Borg obviously took it to heart. His iceberg image was firmly in place by the time he arrived with a flourish on the world stage. All his furious desire to win was channelled into the controlled aggression of his tennis. His ability to remain unruffled under intense pressure is part of sporting legend. It was because of that wonderful temperament that he could win the fifth set of the 1980 Wimbledon final after losing that epic tie-break to McEnroe. Who but Borg could have shrugged off such a calamity

It is often remarked that professional snooker, for all its pressures, is almost always played in a sporting, even gentlemanly spirit. So it is, and it is a credit to the players. There is no place in snooker for petty gamesmanship, let alone any boorish displays of bad temper or angry dissent. In any event, such is the need for titter concentration that real anger is invariably self-destructive. You cannot take your anger out on the balls, as a boxer can on his opponent, although even here it is reckoned that an angry boxer is in great peril against a cool opponent.

Cliff Thorburn would be able to confirm the shattering effects of anger, however ruefully, As well as being amongst the very finest of players, Thorburn is a true gentleman of the game. It may be, as Higgins put it memorably, that he grinds his opponents down, but he does so with unfailing courtesy and not infrequent touches of good humour, as well as with masterful technique. More than anything else, and more than anybody else in the game, he is famed for his competitive qualities that steely concentration, that courage in adversity, the refusal to accept defeat from an apparently hopeless position, that rare ability actually to believe the cliche about the match not being over until the conclusive ball disappears from the table. One could carry on indefinitely about Thorburn's brave fighting qualities. You will have heard such tributes countless times from television commentators and his rival players. You will have seen him salvage matches from seemingly impossible positions, almost by willpower alone. He is, in fact, the ultimate competitor, and in that sense the sporting professional *par excellence..*

An on-camera clash

Anyone who possesses such a will of iron is unlikely to be a placid person. Thorburn is far from placid. No one who has looked at that craggy face would be surprised to know that he has his share of temper. He is not on a particularly short fuse, as world-class competitors go, but he is none the less on a fuse. In a bad mood, in a darkened alley, he is not a man you would especially care to meet, And if you were playing snooker against him, you would not go out of your way to provoke him. On one televised occasion, Alex Higgins did provoke him, not intentionally, it must be said, because Higgins has far too much faith in his own genius to mess about with cheap gamesmanship. But provoke Thorburn he did.

The circumstances are irrelevant to the point of this story, but for those who did not see it, this is what happened. Thorburn was awarded a free ball after a Higgins foul, nominated it and played it. The referee called foul stroke. Some freak of acoustics had prevented him from hearing Thorburn nominate the ball, and admittedly Thorburn had spoken on the quiet side. But his voice had carried to the live audience, and, as countless replays attested, to the television audience as well. It is therefore indisputable that his shot was perfectly legitimate, and the foul call against him a mistake. It was an injustice, and an important one because both frame and match were finely poised.

Thorburn's initial reaction was naturally one of stunned disbelief. How had he fouled? When the referee explained that he had heard no call, Thorburn immediately turned to Higgins for assistance. Had he heard? Higgins, doubtless lost in thoughts of his own, looked perplexed. For whatever mystifying reasons Thorburn's words had failed to reach the referee's ears, they had failed to reach his too.

Now had Higgins had more presence of mind, easy to say for an uninvolved spectator, he would have realized at once that Thorburn must surely have nominated the ball he had so patently played on. Moreover, it was unthinkable that Thorburn could be lying which a false claim would directly imply. In other words, Thorburn just had to be in the right. Having grasped that fundamental, inescapable truth, the obvious response would surely have been to come to Thorburn's aid to ask the referee to reverse his decision, which he would have done on such a request. That is what Thorbum wanted Higgins to do, no more, no less. That would have defused things instantly. The incident would have struck everyone as a bit comical a jest at the referee's expense. A bit of light relief in a tense match.

Instead, Higgins just looked dumbfounded. He appeared not to grasp the situation. His look of wide-eyed bewilderment was as transparent as Thorburn's mounting distress. What on earth was going on? The referee had called a foul. It was nothing to do with him. Why was Thorburn getting so steamed up? And getting steamed up he most certainly was. In the sense that it ever happens, steam was coming out of his ears. Thorburn nearly exploded, not in that childish, whining, self-pitying way that some tennis players do with monotonous regularity, but as perfectly mature, strong-minded people do when they know they are victims of a monstrous miscarriage of justice. Such was Thorburn's visible rage that it is remarkable how well he managed to restrain himself. He was completely beside himself, yet he did not scream the house down and he did not throttle Higgins, which Higgins and a few million viewers must have thought on the cards as they witnessed such awesome fury..

The fatal effects of anger

What he did do was tamely surrender the match. It was way beyond even Thorburn's formidable powers of concentration to put the incident out of his mind and get on with the matter in hand. There could have been no better revenge than to punish his opponent at the table. However, by becoming maddened he had ruined his chances. No one's emotional resources are inexhaustible, and Thorburn had drawn on his too heavily. His concentration was out of the window, and his game could only follow. There are two morals to this story. First, nominate your ball loudly enough to be heard by the referee. The second moral is rather more serious: If you lose control, you lose.

It does not follow from this that you should go out of your way to achieve an ice-cool demeanor. There is nothing wrong with displaying a bit of emotion, although in matchplay you should be careful not to do so in a way that would disturb your opponent. Anger with yourself, when you have made a mess of things, is not only normal, it can be positively beneficial. You will never get anywhere if you are tolerant of your mistakes. On the contrary, you should be your own sternest critic. You know when you have done something stupid, and you should not let yourself get away with it. Give yourself a strict lecture. If that involves cursing yourself under your breath, go right ahead and curse yourself under your breath. On the other hand, do not expect too much of yourself. At least make your opponent beat you rather than beat yourself through frustration.

Depending upon your natural temperament, you will be more or less inclined to display openly your annoyance with yourself. Some players find it a distraction to do so, preferring at all times to keep themselves on a tight rein. No matter how badly he has botched a shot. Steve Davis never allows himself more than a slight, rueful shake of the head, and not very often that. He prefers to mask his emotions behind that familiar impassive facade. That is the image he chooses to present to the world, and he cares nothing for the fact that many observers would warm more to him if he appeared a little looser, a little 'more human'. He probably considers that his demeanor gives him some psychological advantage against some of his opponents, but that, of course, is their problem. They are all after his scalp and he is perfectly entitled to use any fair means to protect that scalp.

Other players find it helps, more than it hurts, to keep the bottle not so tightly corked, It is very easy to tighten up physically during play, under pressure, and they know that to do so is fatal. For them, it is essential to let off a little steam now and then. Their display of annoyance with themselves acts as a safety-value. That great champion of the 1950s and 60s, John Pulman, falls into this category, and he relates an amusing incident about it.

He was involved in an important match with Fred Davis, and lie was playing badly. Nothing would go right. Davis would let him in with a chance, but after two or three pots he would break down. Pulman was getting really incensed about his bad form, angry that he was letting the match slip away through sheer incompetence. After one particular blunder, he could contain himself no longer. He stormed off through the doors and into the manager's office, Where he proceeded to blow his top, against himself, of course.

There was a system whereby a buzzer in the manager's office would recall a player when his opponent broke down, and Pulman was just nicely settled into his tirade when the buzzer sounded. He was amazed by this, because he had left Davis in such a good position that a really big break seemed inevitable. But Davis had obviously broken down early on. Pulman swept back to the fray, but as he bounded into the hall he was greeted with a hail of laughter. When he looked at the table, Pulman could see nothing to laugh about. He was comprehensively snookered snookered in behind the brown in such a way that even if he managed to escape and hit a red, he was virtually certain to let Davis in for a winning break. He did just that, and Davis serenely polished off the frame.

Why that burst of laughter, Pulman demanded to know, as he and Davis went off for the interval? The genial Davis explained. Having messed up his position on the break, he had just trickled up to the brown for that deadly snooker. As he returned to his seat, just a split second before Pulman hurtled through the doors, he had remarked to the crowd: 'Fasten your safety-belts.'

Regardless of how you manage to deal with tension and pressure, you must never allow yourself to lose concentration. You must concentrate from beginning to end, no mean feat in a long match, but you must discipline yourself to do it. At the higher levels of play, a single lapse in concentration can prove fatal. In a friendly game with an equal, it can turn the scales. You must concentrate when you are not at the table as much as when you are. Always watch your opponent at play. There are two reasons for this. First, you may discover his weaknesses, and then go on to exploit them when it is your turn to play. Second, it helps to keep distracting thoughts at bay.

Play positive snooker

You must adopt and retain a positive attitude to playing snooker. Snooker is a game of attack and defence, subtly blended depending upon the circumstances as they evolve during the course of play. However, it is always a positive game, whether the circumstances at any particular stage favour an offensive or defensive stroke. A killing safety shot is every bit as positive as a winning pot..

It is impossible in the pages of a book to give specific advice for the specific situations that you will encounter in the course of your snooker-playing career, but you may find a few general comments helpful. Safety play is a vital aspect of the game, but do not make a fetish of it. Insomuch as snooker can be reduced to a single, bedrock element, it is about potting balls. Do not get into the habit of declining reasonable potting opportunities just because you might miss them. Players who do that will never make much progress. This is not to say that you should throw caution to the winds as you step to the table. You should not make unreasonable demands on your potting skill, and you should not despise good opportunities to make life difficult for your opponent. But, most of the time, at any level of snooker, he best way to discomfort your opponent is to run away from him on the scoreboard. Knock in a good break early on in a frame and you are in business.

You will feel confident and your opponent will feel pressure. Knock in another later on and you will probably win the frame. Keep applying that sort of pressure and you both demoralize and intimidate your opponent. That is really what snooker is all about.

You might think from your experience of watching televised snooker that not all the players adopt such an approach. You would be wrong. They all do, from 'Whirlwind' White to 'Steady Eddie' Charlton. Of course White looks thrilling in attack, and Charlton sometimes dour in defence. White is the better potter. Most experts would say, indeed do say, that he is the most naturally gifted potter the game has ever seen. That being so, it means that he realistically sees reasonable potting opportunities where others, just as realistically, do not. Simply trying to out-pot White would be to fall into the trap of playing him at his own game the game at which he is best, although he has had some marvellous shoot-outs with another gifted young potter, Kirk Stevens. His opponents beat him, when they do, by playing their own game, at their own pace. They play within themselves, as they should. But they all play aggressively, as they must do to stand any chance of winning at that level. At your level, the same truth holds.

Not only will excessive devotion to safety play inhibit your progress as a player, it will stifle your enjoyment, Snooker is, after all, only a game, and games are supposed to be fun. Bold players are bound to have more fun than timid ones. It is a lovely feeling to make a difficult pot, and how can you experience that feeling if you always duck the challenge? How wretched the game would become if you scuttled for safety the whole time, priding yourself on the fact that while you may not be scoring, your opponent is making no headway either.

The professionals see it the same way, even with so much at stake. A cautious attitude is not what stirred them to take up the game in the first place, develop such a passion for it and set out to conquer the world. Griffiths could be speaking for all of them when he says that he can bear to play an attacking game and lose, even if the loss is directly caused by a risky attacking shot that fails to come off. But he absolutely detests losing if he has been put on the defensive and has allowed himself to remain there without striking out boldly for victory. Whenever you find negative thoughts creeping into your mind, as of course they will, try to remember the old adage: 'Fortune favours the brave.' Or the new one: 'Go for it! Win or lose, that is the way to play.

9

THE SNOOKER BOOM

The early Seventies were to see the presentation of snooker transformed from a low-key, low-budget affair in obscure venues to a professionally staged sporting spectacle. Television discovered a popular formula for professional snooker one frame sudden death at the same time as television programmes began to be shown in colour. Since snooker is the only game in which colour is an intrinsic part of the rules, this change had a spectacular effect. The first programme of "Pot Black", the progenitor of many television snooker series, was seen on BBC2 on July 23, 1969. It was a series which was to introduce snooker to sections of the community who had previously scarcely known of its existence. It was to make reputations for those players who appeared on it, which reached far beyond the traditional bounds of the snooker world. A player invited to appear on "Pot Black" usually found himself in much greater demand for the club exhibitions which still yielded the bulk of his income.

As sponsorship became an accepted part of the game, sponsors and their advisers tried to ensure that they received value for their investment. Sponsored tournaments, particularly those for which a sponsor engaged a public relations consultancy, therefore tended to be more efficiently run and better publicised. The legalisation of gaming machines, one-armed bandits, in clubs sparked a revolution: as Jack Rea, who had slogged round the club exhibition circuit in the dark days of the Fifties and early Sixties put it: "A lot of clubs were tin shacks when I first played there. When I went back in the Seventies, I looked for a tin shack and found a palace standing in its place."

The clubs, then, had more money to play with but ultimately all depended on the new cast of players which was offered to the public. Three of these, Spencer, Reardon and Higgins, all of whom were to win the championship', were to be outstanding figures of these years.

Spencer's golden years were from 1969-71. His long potting, dazzling screw shots and general lack of inhibition in his play made him unquestionably no. I at this time despite the occasional reverse. Indeed, even when Reardon began his four-year tenure of the world title in 1973, Spencer had the better record in non championship tournaments only to suffer a series of failures in the championship itself. On his return from Australia with a then record first prize cheque of £2,333 for the 1970 championship in his pocket, Spencer launched into, in January 1971, and won, the first Park Drive £2,000 tournament, a round robin event in which he, Owen, Pulman and Williams played each other three times In seven-frame matches before the top two played off for the first two prizes of £750 and £550

The Park Drive event was not only snooker's first whiff of tournament sponsorship outside the world championship since the *News of the World* tournament but the initial involvement in the sport of West and Nally, a fresh, young London public relations firm specialising in the rapidly developing world of sports sponsorship. The concept of this tournament was original: 18 one-night stands in clubs with the final, also in a club, on television, the first professional tournament match to be televised for over 15 years. The involvement of West and Nally was also to lead to the first lengthy and level-headed appraisal from the outside of what snooker had to offer as a public entertainment and where its lamentably out-of-date methods of presentation had to be improved.

Peter West, a television commentator and compere of wide experience, and Patrick Nally, a boundlessly energetic motivator and ideas man, improved snooker's relationship with television sports departments and established it as a sport in which a sponsor might extract a reasonable commercial return, particularly in the fields of tobacco and drink. It was the first time snooker had a high-powered, media-orientated outfit behind it and its role in the snooker boom of the 1970s has never been sufficiently acknowledged.

Higgins, meanwhile, was about to burst through to the top with all the irresistible crest of a wave force his nickname "Hurricane" implies. The draw for the world championship, made in February 1971—the final was played in February 1972— placed Higgins in one of the qualifying sections. He was to have to play six matches to win the title.

Spencer won the first Park Drive £2,000; Reardon rounded off his win in the Park Drive £600, an event specially devised for Yorkshire Television, with a break of 127, the highest thus far seen on the screen; John Dunning, 11 times Yorkshire amateur champion, brought off the shock of the 1971 season by beating Spencer 13-10 in the Willie Smith Trophy in Leeds before Higgins beat him easily in the final; Higgins and Spencer played to packed houses in a series of £200 challenge matches; Reardon beat Spencer 4-3 on the final black after needing a snooker on the pink in the final of the second Park Drive £2,000; and Spencer, with the help of the livelier Canadian ball, Vitalite, and the more generous Canadian pockets, made 29 centuries and 60 breaks over 80 in 98 frames against Cliff Thorburn in Calgary and Edmonton.

It was a visit which opened Thorburn's eyes to a world beyond the pool rooms of Canada and the John Spencer United States which had been his habitat for almost ten years but it was also one which left Spencer exhausted, for on his return he struggled past Charlton with great difficulty in the world semi-final—a match which carried a personal sidestake of £750 before winning the third Park Drive £2,000 with a 4-3 win over Higgins the evening before they started their world final in the unpretentious concert hall of Selly Park British Legion, Birmingham.

Higgins had survived his semifinal against Williams only by winning the last of the 61 frames, casting away frames when he was in a winning position and winning them from losing positions with equal abandon. Only a little while before he had ended Rea's 21-year tenure of the Irish professional title by beating him 28-12 with the aid of a fabulous 9-0 third session and beat Reardon handsomely in a big match at the City Hall, Sheffield. Spencer was nevertheless a clear favourite to retain the title but Higgins played with sublime confidence to become, a few days after his 23rd birthday, the youngest ever champion. A miner's strike and the consequent power failures contributed not only to the capacity afternoon attendances but to a bizarre incident on the second evening when, with conventional lighting out of action and no heating in the room on this cold February night, the players agreed to continue under the dull and inadequate lighting produced by a mobile generator. Amazingly, the first three frames lasted only 35 minutes. The hall bulged with the crowd accommodated on seats placed on stacked beer crates, used as a rough form of tiered seating, or hanging precariously from any point of vantage. Snooker was simply not used to the idea of paying customers being so keen to see a match. Even Fleet Street sports editors conceded that there was a degree of interest in the contest.

Not all the referees were up to such an important occasion. After two ghastly howlers, the unprecedented —and never repeate—step was taken of appointing "linesmen", one sitting on either side of the table, to assist adjudication when the referee was in doubt or to settle appeals.

Amidst it all, Higgins missed no more than two pots in the entire week that he might reasonably have been expected to get and an unforgettable 60 win in the Thursday evening session put him very much in the driver's seat. Spencer fought hard and made the only two centuries of the match but Higgins was not to be denied. He clinched the title early in the final session, 37-32, and snooker was never the same again. His victory convinced West and Nally of snooker's wider potentialities. Under their direction, the fourth Park Drive £2,000 was staged in October when Spencer, in front of a crowd of 2,000 at Belle Vue, Manchester, beat Higgins 5-3 for the £750 first prize., his fourth first prize out of the four £2,000 and two £600 tournaments which Park Drive had sponsored.

This crystallised Nally's burgeoning scheme to convert the World Professional Championship from an unwieldy event, lasting several months in different venues with no continuity of interest and scant media interest into a lavishly staged, Wimbledon-style spectacle with play taking place on eight tables in different arenas in the same large venue. With the sponsorship of Park Drive, West and Nally promoted at City Exhibition Halls, Manchester—to their immediate financial loss but the game's ultimate gain—a championship condensed into a fortnight, with £8,000 prize money, television coverage, public bars and, for the first time, public restaurants, a Ladbroke betting tent and carefully nurtured press coverage from every national newspaper.

The publicity bandwagon, already rolling, gathered momentum when a documentary, "Hurricane Higgins'", reached 25th place in the joint ITV/BBC ratings for the week. It was a film which showed that a lonely wait for a train and some rather desperate tinselly gaiety was as much a part of this young genius' life as an incredible exhibition at a Northern workingmen's club or a serious match with Spencer at Wallasey Town Hall. It was no public relations exercise but it helped confirm Higgins in the minds of a great section of the uncommitted public as the only snooker player it had ever heard of. His partiality to wine, women and gambling, heavily publicised in an opportunist spread in the *Sunday People* and elsewhere, and his propensity for getting involved in disturbances, coupled with his dash, skill and bravado, made him a popular hero. At the table he behaved immaculately. Away from it he made it quite clear, self-destructively so at times, that he did not give a damn for anyone or anything. West and Nally attempted to manage him but retired badly bruised.

The publicity build-up for the 1973 championship was centred round Higgins, not least because it was easy to write colourfully about him. He was seeded to meet Spencer in the final but those who expected a repeat of the 1972 final or the epic £1,000-a-side struggle at Radcliffe Town Hall, which Spencer won 38-37, were disappointed as neither reached the final.

There was trouble in Higgins's first match when he arrived more than *20* minutes late for his evening session with Houlihan. In the absence of precise tournament regulations, the tournament director, Bruce Donkin, ticked off Higgins in no uncertain manner but Higgins, after a placatory speech had been unenthusiastically received, won the crowd over within five minutes with a dazzling break of 78.

His quarter-final against Fred Davis uniquely included a stoppage for rain. Even in Manchester this was a bit thick, but the position was duly marked, the covers were put on and play ceased until the offending leak in the roof had been plugged. The clash of styles between the impetuous, brilliant Higgins and the calm, reflective, steady Davis, not to mention the element of what many saw as Young Upstart versus a member of snooker's royal family, erupted to a nerve-wrenching climax. Davis led 14-12, missed a pink which would have put him one up with two to go, and went down 16-14 as Higgins played with all his death or glory bravery to snatch a semifinal place. This, though, was the end of the road as Charlton won the first six frames of their semifinal and in the same inexorable manner ground out a 23-9 win. The Higgins bubble had burst.

While this was happening, the other semifinal seemed to be proceeding quietly towards a routine win for Spencer, who led Reardon 19-12 and then missed an easy black which would have put him 20-14 ahead. Instead, Reardon pulled back to only four behind and added the remaining three frames of the penultimate session to trail 18-19 at the interval. Reardon's revival had coincided with the end of the Higgins-Charlton match, and the spectators flooded into the hitherto half-empty arena where he and Spencer were playing. More sensitive to atmosphere, perhaps, than any of the other leading players, Reardon's adrenalin was now well and truly flowing and after innumerable thrills and vicissitudes, he clinched victory in the deciding frame, 23-22. This traumatic psychological blow seemed to affect Spencer deeply: he won many matches and many tournaments and regained the championship in 1977 but all without recapturing more than fleetingly the easy confidence and sublime form of his greatest years.

Reardon also suffered a reaction—merely a temporary one—when, next day, he lost the first seven frames of the final, another absorbing match in which

Reardon's flair and wider range of shots were pitted against Charlton's dogged consistency. Reardon led 17-13 after the fourth session and kept in front to 27-25 until the eighth session broke the pattern into which the match had settled. After only a few minutes under the blinding, newly installed television lights it was obvious that Charlton could see but Reardon could not. Three frames went with ludicrous ease to the Australian before Reardon's protests led to two of the largest floodlights, which in any event were needed only to illuminate the crowd, were switched off. Further discussion took place at the mid-session interval during which Reardon was able to compose himself. He emerged to win four of the five remaining frames of the day to lead 31-29 and, as if conscious the crisis of the match had passed, forged steadily ahead to win 38-32.

Higgins, apparently temperamentally unfitted to cope either with success or failure, went to Australia where he was thrown out of one club after calling Norman Squire "an old no-hoper" he was allowed in again after writing an abject apology on a piece of toilet paper and out of an hotel for wrecking his room. A projected tour of India lasted only one day for, after starting his first exhibition at Bombay Gymkhana with a break of 109, he so offended the members of this gentlemanly club by his drinking, the stripping off of his shirt and his insulting behaviour that the B.A. and C.C. of India, his hosts, put him on the next plane home. A childish threat not to complete his commitments in the "Pot Black" series recorded at the end of 1972 was not carried out but was punished by his omission from the 1973 and subsequent series. Wild, uncontrollable, wilful, Higgins seemed bent on self-destruction. Reardon, the new champion, predictably flourished. He toured India at short notice to repair the damage done by Higgins to professional snooker's reputation; made 65 public centuries in a four-month tour of South Africa; and compiled a second 147 maximum shortly after his return. Snooker Promotions, the sudsidiary West and Nally had set tip to tackle their increasing snooker commitment, organised, with Ladbroke sponsorship, two gala dinner snooker evenings at the Cafe Royal in 1973 and 1974, and, most important, obtained a valuable new sponsor, Norwich Union, whose tournament at the Piccadilly Hotel brought big-time snooker back to London.

Though it did not justify its billing as a World Open Championship, the field was internationally representative both of the professional and amateur sides of the game except that Reardon chose not to compete and Williams and Davis were engaged on the Watnev exhibition series which occupied a good part of their British winters from 1968-76. Higgins, whose brilliance had grown more and more fitful., fell 8-2 to Spencer in one semifinal while, more surprisingly, Pulman, who had done nothing of note since 1970, overcame Charlton 8-3 in the other. The final provided exciting television for Spencer led 6-2 and, repeating his semifinal blunder against Reardon in the world championship, missed a chance to make it 7-2. This was all the encouragement Pulman needed for, revelling in the mounting tension, he recovered to 7-7 and looked like winning the decider before he missed a not too difficult green.

Spencer, who won £1,500 to Pulman's £750, also took part in another Snooker Promotions exercise, the televised Norwich Union Transatlantic Challenge, the first serious attempt in Britain to establish any meaningful contact between the hitherto utterly self-contained worlds of snooker and American pool, though Williams and Charlton had both played pool in the United States. Steve Mizerak, the United States Open pool champion, predictably beat Spencer 3-0 at pool and, rather less predictably, beat him 2-1 at snooker which, even though Spencer was not buckling down with maximum determination, indicated that the top American pool players possessed the basic cuemanship, even allowing for vast differences in the size of balls, pockets and tables, to become snooker players of good professional standard. Mlizerak's visit stimulated British interest in pool. Indeed, pool was to become one of the great growth areas in the 1970s though, ironically, this growth was to occur primarily in pubs, amusement arcades, hotel foyers and in other places not otherwise associated with snooker tables. Save in the fact that it may have accustomed some people to using a cue who subsequently progressed to snooker, the growth of pool in Britain was to have no discernible influence on snooker.

West and Nally founded another subsidiary, Mister Billiards, to sell pool tables and equipment and with an enterprising snooker and pool stand at the Ideal Home Exhibition on which they staged matches featuring Spencer, then a director of Mister Billiards, and other top professionals, again contributed to the rising tide of interest in the game. Cliff Thorburn, resident professional for the show, recorded a four-frame sequence of breaks of 94, 100, 146 and 130 though in exhibitions elsewhere Spencer and Higgins both went one better by completing century breaks in four consecutive frames. But disappointments were round the corner. Park Drive increased the prize money for the 1974 world championship but the vast, concrete floored, aircraft hangar-like hall at Belle Vue, Manchester, did not prove a successful choice of venue. This might not have mattered if the main box office attractions had not lost early but, as it was, Reardon retained his title with consummate ease.

Spencer went out in his first match 15-13 to Mans; Charlton did likewise 15-13 to Dunning; and Higgins lost an epic quarterfinal 15-14 to the 61-year-old Davis, Just recuperating from his second heart attack. Higgins led 13-9 before, at 13-11, he was controversially called for a push stroke, a decision which was instrumental in Davis pulling up to 12-13. Higgins led 14-12 but Davis, showing remarkable stamina, won the last three frames to win 15-14.

The modern world championship format, cramming into a fortnight a number of matches which in the old days would have taken several weeks, threw additional physical and mental stress on the participants so it was not too surprising that Davis was submerged 15-3 in one semi-final by Reardon while Graham Miles, who had sprung from obscurity by coming into "Pot Black" as a late replacement for Davis and winning it not only that year but the following year, beat Dunning and Williams to qualify from the other half. Miles, a very unorthodox sighter of the ball in that his cue runs not under his chin but under his left ear, had displayed, notably in a 131 semi-final break, much touch and positional skill but his inspiration had burnt out by the time he contested the final and Reardon won very easily 22-12.

Immediately after the tournament, Snooker Promotions presented to the W.P.B.S.A. a schedule of their ambitious plans for an international tournament circuit, only for these to be rejected so vehemently that West and Nally's interest in snooker was henceforth to be confined to servicing tournaments in a public relations capacity for sponsors they had obtained. What the company had achieved for snooker became a matter not for graditude but envy, jealousy and distrust. The 1975 world championship was awarded to Eddie Charlton Promotions; Park Drive disappeared from snooker; and the niggling and internecine strife which had so disfigured the game in the past, disfigured it again. Charlton, who dominated the Australian scene in every way, and Williams, chairman of the W.P.B.S.A., emerged as the dominant personalities of the professional scene and, because there were personal differences with Bruce Donkin, who had by now become the day-to-day director of business at Snooker Promotions and Mister Billiards, a parting of the ways was almost inevitable.

Though this contretemps retarded the prospect of a full tournament circuit, a new tournament immediately after the 1974 championship was to become, through its initial success, a permanent feature of the calendar. Pontins, the holiday camp empire where Spencer, Reardon and David Taylor had long-standing contracts to play summer exhibitions, organised at their Prestatyn camp a Festival of Snooker which consisted not only of an eight-man professional event but an Open where 25 amateur qualifiers joined the professionals in the last 32. Reardon beat Spencer 109 to win the professional event, but there was a surprise when Doug Mountjoy, then only an unpredictable if talented amateur, took advantage of the handicap to win the Open, beating both Reardon and Spencer.

It was an event which emphasised the snooker world's intimate, democratic qualities. The holiday-makers mixed for the week with the stars of their sport, some of them earning a chance for glory and cash against the big names, all of them having the opportunity to watch top-class matches and talk snooker as much as they liked. To a degree unparalleled in the snooker world, it brought the snooker family closer together.

Jim Williamson's Northern Snooker Centre in Leeds, a purpose-built snooker club with a match arena, staged its first big event, the £3,000 Watneys Open, in the latter part of the year when Higgins, who had learnt a great deal about safety play and the less spectacular arts of the game to replace the loss of the fine edge of his potting ability, beat Reardon 13-11 and Davis I7-11 to take the £1,000 first prize.

As four-man and eight-man tournaments proliferated, Spencer retained the Norwich Union Open title with a 10-9 win over Reardon which again revealed his difficulty in clinching winning positions. Spencer led 8-4 but was caught at 8-8 and was eventually indebted to a fluke to give him a crucial advantage in the deciding frame. Reardon, just returned from an exhausting four-week tour of Australia and New Zealand, suffered the effects of jet lag during the tournament and in so doing made it clear that snooker players had now joined other sportsmen in travelling hectically about the globe in pursuit of their profession. He beat Higgins 9-8 in a spellbinding semifinal while Thorburn, who had beaten Davis and Pulman, demonstrated his improvement by extending Spencer to 9-7 in the other.

Despite packed houses and abundant television coverage, Norwich Union withdrew their sponsorship but the snooker calendar gained a valuable new event again through West and Nally—when another Gallaher brand, Benson and Hedges, backed a Masters tournament. Though later housed at the New London Theatre, and later still at the Wembley Conference Centre, the initial Benson and Hedges Masters, was first held at the West Centre Hotel in an atmosphere of plush and glitter which established the event, as intended, as the Ascot of the snooker world. Spencer and Reardon again reached the final though Reardon got there only 5-4 on the final pink against Williams, who had beaten Higgins.

The final followed a familiar pattern of Spencer leading and Reardon equalising until, leading 8-6, Reardon looked a certain winner. The standard was poor, perhaps because, night after night, the leading players were now experiencing more pressure, more general wear and tear on the nervous system, than in any previous era. Eventually Spencer levelled at 8-8 and held a commanding lead in the decider only to throw it away. Reardon then had a golden chance to win but was distracted on the crucial pink by a bevy of Benson and Hedges promotion girls rising in their seats, presumably to be on hand for the prize-giving ceremony. The frame ended in a tie before Spencer somehow summoned one of his best pots of the session to despatch the extra black for the £2,000 first prize.

Since Spencer and Reardon were clearly two of the top or probably the top two players, there was uproar when the seedings for the 1975 World Professional Championship, playing in various venues all over Australia, placed Reardon, at no. 1, and Spencer, at 8, to meet in the quarterfinals. The fact that the draw was made contrary to W.P.B.S.A. conditions was allowed to pass and it did not escape the attention of the cognoscenti that not only Reardon and Spencer but Higgins were all in the opposite half of the draw to the promoter, Charlton.

In quality, the quarterfinal was one of the best matches Reardon and Spencer played, countless frames turning on a single half chance or being won from 50 or 60 behind. Trailing 16-17, Reardon won the next three frames to win 19-17 and, from 10-10, beat Higgins 19-14 in the semi. In the opposite half, Dennis Taylor, a young Blackburn-based Irishman, made his first significant impact on the championship by beating Mans 15-12, Davis 15-14 and Gary Owen 19-9 but had to endure a choppy plane trip from Sydney to Brisbane on the morning of his semi-final against Charlton and never recovered from a poor start.

It was an extraordinary final. Reardon led 16-8 but Charlton strung together the next nine frames to lead 17-16. It was 22-20 to Reardon but, when Charlton led 28-23, the title seemed certain to go to Australia for the first time. However, the match began to turn when Reardon potted a daring pink to keep in the match at 25-29. When Charlton missed a frame ball brown of the type he rarely misses before losing the next frame of the final session by going in-off the black, his recovery gathered momentum. Reardon extended his winning streak to seven to lead 30-29 before the excited crowd in the Nunawading Basketball Stadium saw Charlton equalise at 30-30. After a tense opening to the decider, when the Australian held the initiative, Reardon fashioned a break of 62 to give him the £4,000 first prize and his third consecutive title.

A week later, Reardon was back on the other side of the world, winning both the professional and Open sections at Pontins and another £2,000 but it was in 1975 that the professional game suffered a chaotic disruption through the involvement of 'Q' Promotions, a management and promotions company run by Maurice Hayes, at that time also the vice-chairman of the B. & S.C.C. Hayes began promisingly by organising several small professional tournaments and handling bookings for a number of players. When he obtained the sponsorship of W.D. and H.O. Wills, under their Embassy banner, for the 1976 world championship, some went as far as to hall him as the game's new Messiah, but as his involvement escalated so did he find it more difficult to control. There were confusions over bookings and in the pre-organisation of the championship despite ever more desperate efforts to hold things together.

The three Embassy-sponsored subsidiary events to the championship, a women's Open, an invitation amateur tournament and an open-to-all amateur tournament, all good ideas in themselves, proved to the sponsors more trouble than they were worth. The decision to run the top half of the championship draw at Middlesbrough Town Hall and the bottom half and the final at Wythenshawe Forum proved administratively unwieldy and dissipated the unity of place which had been such a virtue of the championships organised by West and Nally.

Having taken the £2,000 first prize in the Benson and Hedges Masters by beating Charlton, excitingly, 554 and Miles, easily, 7-3, Reardon was in a class of his own at Middlesbrough where the hasty and incomplete blackout, the clatter of spectators moving from one arena to another or to the bar or toilet and other small but irritating imperfections claimed most of the press attention. At Wythenshawe, too, the championship began controversially when Charlton claimed, correctly, that the pockets of the table on which he was playing Pulman were larger than standard. This was put right—Charlton made a 137 break in this match while Spencer made a 138 on the other table but criticism of the table conditions was to be redoubled when one table was taken out and the other re-set for the semi-final and final.

Higgins, still wayward and unpredictable in a personal sense, had meanwhile started to regain some of the ground he bad lost since his title win in 1972. Still willing to chance his arm, but more balanced and technically more complete, he had beaten Spencer in the final of a £2,000 Open at the Castle Club, Southampton, and had, amazingly, added to his four 147 maximums a 146 in which, profiting initially from taking a free ball as the "extra" red, he had taken, in addition, the usual 15 reds and all the colours, the first such clearance recorded. In the championship Higgins was on the brink of defeat as Thorburn confirmed his emergence as a world class player to lead 14-12 but then a surge of inspiration, backed by some luck, carried Higgins to a 15-14 victory. After leading 14-12,

Higgins also needed the last frame to beat Spencer 15-14 and, to the delight of some of snooker's most vociferous supporters, won a third close finish, 20-18 against Charlton, to reach the final.

The final began farcically, the glare and dazzle from the newly-installed television lighting being altogether unacceptable. Reardon, who had the additional disadvantage of having played all his previous matches in Middlesbrough, fumed visibly as he slipped to a 2-4 deficit at the first interval. The champion won six of the seven evening frames to lead 8-5 but there was more trouble on the second afternoon when Reardon, with every justification, complained bitterly about the running of the table. Attempts were made to put things right in the interval—by which time Higgins was again ahead 10-9—and Reardon, shrewdly playing a cautious and limited game despite his far-from-happy state of mind, again won the evening session 6-1 to lead 15-11. Higgins won the first two frames the following day but a failure at a shot he attempted left-handed cost him the next frame. This miss and the loss of the next two frames from winning positions virtually signalled the end of the contest and Reardon's 27-16 win earned him a new record first prize of £6,000.

Within weeks, though, 'Q' Promotions had folded up. Some of the good they did lingered on—preeminently bringing Embassy into snooker—and in general they can be said to have added to rather than diminished the anarchy within the game.

In contrast to the brisk movement between the amateur and professional ranks of the preceding two years, the 1969-75 period was to be dominated in the amateur world by three players, two of whom did riot seriously consider such a change, partly because in 1972 the B. & S.C.C. removed all restrictions on amateurs accepting fees or prize money. A professional thus came to be defined as a member of the W.P.B.S.A. or one who "declares himself a professional". In practice this meant that an amateur could earn as much as any but the top eight or ten professionals, so it was pointless to turn professional. Ray Edmonds, Sid Hood and Jonathan Barron between them filled ten of the 14 places in the English finals of this period. Edmonds, manager of a painting and decorating merchants in Grimsby, Barron, an antique dealer and souvenir shop proprietor in Mevagissey, and Hood, a Grimsby docker with a particular relish for the social life of amateur snooker, contested some gripping matches.

Edmonds, after four unsuccessful appearances in the Northern final, recovered from 3-7 to beat Barron 11-9 in the 1969 final at Grimsby, the year in which a popular London competitor, Bill Smith, died during his match against Houlihan in the Southern section at Great Windmill Street. It was also the year of the first official amateur snooker international, instigated by Wales, who received England in a special match at Port Talbot to mark the investiture of the Prince of Wales. The success of the venture led to triangular series with Scotland the following year, with the Republic of Ireland making it a: four-cornered contest a year later.

In 1970, Barron recorded the first of his hat-trick of titles when he beat Hood 11-10. Both men went to Edinburgh for the 1970 World Amateur Championship and both, after some early alarms, won their groups to contest the final with Barron winning a somewhat scrappy final 11-7. Having made two successful defences of his English title, 11-9 against Doug French at Harringay and 11-9 against Edmonds at Truro, he defended his world title in Wales in what was officially the 1972 championship but which actually finished in the early days of 1973.

The championship was originally scheduled for Sri Lanka, but the new World Council, the one-nation, one-vote body which had taken control of the World Amateur Championships, had adopted a rule whereby "the host national association must invite entries from every affiliated national association". However, the government of Sri Lanka not only forbade its nationals to compete in South Africa but refused to allow national associations invite South Africans to compete in events in Sri Lanka. The net result was that Sri Lanka, after a postal vote, was deprived of the right to stage the championship and Wales, at short notice, stepped into the breach.

The popular Jimmy van Rensburg, the acceptance of whose entry the Scottish association had to withdraw at the eleventh hour for the 1970 championship in Edinburgh because of pressure from anti-apartheid interests, came to Wales, as did another South African, Mannie Francisco. The Edinburgh entry, with ten nations represented among the 14 competitors, had been the strongest to date but the 18 competitors from ten nations who competed in Wales were of even higher overall standard. Four round robin groups reduced the field to eight and two more groups of four produced the qualifiers for the knockout semifinals. The dashing 16-stone Indian, Arvind Savur Tornado Fats in some newspapers—looked well set for the final when he led Francisco 4-0 in their 15-frame semi-final at the Sophia Garden Pavilion, Cardiff, although he felt the low temperature so intensely that his bridge hand cramped up with cold, a condition for which he attempted several remedies, among them massaging his hands with whisky. Francisco adopted the correct tactics in slowing the Indian down with liberal doses of safety play and gradually fought his way into the match. At 7-7, Savur potted green, brown, blue but, playing with the rest, wobbled the pink, which would have put him in the final, in the jaws. Francisco took the pink and, after a safety exchange on the black, potted it in a deathly silence to win 8-7.

In the other semi-final, Barron lost his title when Edmonds won a scrappy match 86. Barron, a fine competitor with the knack of potting the really important balls, had often, even in his three-year spell of unbroken success in major events between 1969 and 1972, looked as if the strain of the occasion was about to prove too much for him. Burying his brow in his hands between shots, like a man with a blinding headache, Barron doubtless looked—much like the great Olympic champion Emil Zatopek—much worse than he felt. Nevertheless, much of the strain was real for, after the 1973 English championship, when he lost in the Southern semi-final to Marcus Owen, he retired from championship snooker.

The final provided for Francisco a reversal of his great recovery against Savur for he won the first six frames and led 6-1 overnight. On the resumption, Francisco led 7-2 but Edmonds recovered to 6-8 at the interval by sinking a long bold black for game after Francisco had needed only an easy pink, almost straight across the table, for a 9-5 lead, a blunder which both players subsequently agreed proved to be the crucial point of the match. The South African led 9-6 but Edmonds invariably looked cooler in moments of crisis and won the next four frames. Francisco levelled at 10-10 but Edmonds always had his nose in front in the decider and half an hour after midnight, after the players had occupied the table for 7½ hours that evening, he clinched the match 11-10.

The result, a tribute to Edmonds's heart and determination, was a sadder commentary on Francisco's inability to clinch a winning position which his excellent technique, cue-ball control and tactical acumen had earned. Nevertheless, to have finished second in world championships at both billiards and snooker effectively underlines his claim to be regarded as the outstanding amateur all-rounder of his time.

Edmonds went on to retain the Northern section of the English championship by beating John Virgo 6-4 but the organisation of the national final fell into such disarray that it did not take place in Birmingham until mid-May, by which time Edmonds's inspiration and concentration had faded, and Owen regained the title after not entering for six years. Owen then turned professional but failed to make the impact in the professional championship that he assuredly would have made if he had done so at his peak between 1958 and 1963. The following year, however, Edmonds did win the English title with a comfortable 11-7 over Patsy Fagan, a Putney-based Irishman who typified a new breed of young players which was thriving amidst the general air of high activity in the snooker world by playing money matches against both amateurs and professionals. Under the management and backing then of Peter Careswell and later of George Jackson, Fagan established himself as a fine player in a situation not unlike that which used commonly to exist in boxing when a local businessman-sportsman would take up a local hopeful and, in return for the thrill of involvement and a percentage of earnings, nurture his career.

Another young player, Willie Thorne, who had shown great promise in winning the British boys championship in 1970 and junior championship in 1973 and becoming England's youngest international in 1973, came through by capturing the Southern title in a blaze of glory in 1975 with breaks of 91,71 and 80 in his 8-5 win over Chris Ross. Having beaten him five times out of five, Thorne was expected to beat Hood in the national final at Hull but after winning the first frame with an 86 break he fell victim to the most determined and sustained effort Hood made in his long career. Hood won 11 6 and the 21-year-old Thorne turned professional the following November when, in view of his obvious talent and a defeat of Spencer in an international tournament in Toronto, he was invited to compete in "Pot Black".

Edmonds had retained the World Amateur Championship at the Crofton Airport Hotel, Dublin, in November 1974 in a field inferior to that of 1972. South Africa, whose nomination of Silvino Francisco and Mike Hines had originally been accepted, was forced to withdraw after the Irish Transport and General Workers Union made it clear that their support for the anti-apartheid movement would lead to the event being crippled by industrial action, demonstrations and disruptions.

The field of 18 was divided into two groups. Edmonds, despite losing his opening match 4-3 to Mohammed Lafir, won group A while Alwyn Lloyd, who had won the 1973 and 1974 Welsh championships as Welsh standards of play rose and the organisation of their association began to be geared more to the international game, won group B undefeated. Lloyd, who made breaks of 97 against David Sneddon and 104 against N.J. Rahim, played some of the best snooker of the championship but all this went for naught when he was beaten 4-2 by his compatriot Geoff Thomas, the 1972 Welsh champion, in the quarter-finals.

The system of allowing the top four from each group through to the knockout quarter-finals actually appeared to give a psychological advantage to those who qualified in fourth place. Thomas, for instance, with four defeats, only qualified on frames after a late run and thus played against Lloyd like a man unexpectedly reprieved and with everything to gain and nothing to lose. The same nearly happened to Edmonds, for Lou Condo, the Australian who had finished fourth in the other group, played his best snooker of the tournament to lead 3-1 before the holder won 4-3.

When Edmonds led Thomas 5-2 in the final it looked oddson an early finish but the Welshman recovered to 7-7 at the second interval and again showed his tenacity by converting 7-9 into 9-9. But 'Thomas, it seemed, could not quite picture himself as world champion and, after missing a green with the rest which would have given him a 10-9 lead, he lost this and the following frame for Edmonds, like Gary Owen in 1963 and 1966, to win his second world amateur title.

South Africa's unprecedented offer to pay air fares for one competitor and one delegate from each affiliated country to the World Amateur Championship in Johannesburg in 1976 enabled some of the more impoverished national associations to be represented and others who would have been refused a grant, by their governments to be represented at no cost to themselves. Twenty-four players were divided into three groups with three qualifying from each and two of the third place finishers being drawn by lot to contest a match to reduce the field to eight. India and Sri Lanka were forbidden by their governments to compete but the entry was of high overall quality and the setting, the President Hotel, Johannesburg, lavish.

The tournament was to see the end of England's domination, an out-of-touch Chris Ross finishing fourth in his group, Roy Andrewartha falling 0-4 to the 1975 Welsh champion, Terry Griffiths, in the found before the quarterfinals, and Edmonds going out 5-1 in the quarters to Mifsud, who was to give Malta a world amateur finalist for the first time.

Wales, home international champions in 1975 and 1976, emphasised their rising status on the international scene by supplying a quarter-finalist., Griffiths, and the new champion, Doug Mountjoy, who epitomised a new breed of player which had flourished since the abolition of all restrictions on amateurs accepting prize money or exhibition fees.

Though he had won the Welsh amateur title in 1968, Mountjoy had remained for several years a player whose outstanding natural ability was frequently obscured by inconsistency. Having become the first amateur to win a £1,000 first prize in the first Pontin's Open at Prestatyn in 1974, Mountjoy had played full time without risk of losing his amateur status and won the Pontin's Open again before he went to South Africa.

Mountjoy won all seven of his group matches, making a break of 107 in his 4-1 win over the Maori, Norman Stockman, which, but for a disappointing failure at the last red, looked certain to develop into a new world amateur record.

In the quarter-finals Ron Atkins, who had impressed with a solid, efficient, consistent style reminiscent of his professional compatriot, Charlton—even more so through his courage in overcoming the loss of a leg in a teenage shooting accident—was unlucky enough to find Mountjoy at his most dominating as he clinched a 5-1 win with an 80 break in the last frame. Van Rensburg, a clever tactician, ended visions of an all-Welsh final by beating Griffiths 5-3 and Mifsud squashed Edmond's hopes of a hattrick of titles by beating him 5-1, not a surprising result in view of the Englishman's patchy form throughout the tournament. More surprising in terms of past results was Silvino's 51 win over Mannie, 12 years his senior, in the clash between the Francisco brothers, but whereas Silvino had impressed as an outstanding potter Mannie's always suspect temperament had deteriorated since reaching the 1972 final in Cardiff.

Mifsud, going boldly for every chance, then beat Van Rensburg 8-4 but the final saw Mountjoy outclass him 11-1 just as he had overwhelmed Silvino Francisco 8-2 in the semi. There was no mistaking that Mountjoy was top professional class. Next day, having submitted a postdated application, he became a professional, and Ross and Andrewartha, less successfully, turned a few weeks later.

In his first professional tournament, Mountjoy illustrated how narrow was the gap between top amateur and professional standards when he beat Pulman 4-2, Davis 4-2, Higgins 5-3 and Reardon, in a wonderfully exciting finish, 7-6 on the final pink to win the Benson and Hedges Masters in February 1977.

10

SNOOKER RULES

Snooker is played with twenty two balls, fifteen reds, six different colours and a white cue ball. At the start of a game, the reds are positioned in a triangle above and as close as possible to, but with out touching, the pink which is sitting on its spot. The other coloured balls are on their respective spots as well, while the cue ball is placed anywhere for the first stroke. Thereafter, the cue ball must be played from where it rests on the table except when it has been accidentally potted or been forced off the table.

Points are scored in two ways. The principal means is by potting balls. On each trip to the table a player must first attempt to strike a red. If he pots it he scores one point, and he must then attempt to strike any one of the colours. He must nominate the colour he is attempting to hit, although this rule is ignored where the choice is obvious. If there could be the slightest doubt, he must nominate. Potting the various coloured balls score: yellow (2), green (3), brown (4), blue (5), pink (6), black (7). Whereas potted reds stay down in the pockets, a potted colour is replaced on its spot, and the player must play on another red. If he succeeds in potting another red, he is back on the colours, my colour, and so on until he fails to pot a ball. Then it is the next player's turn. The game proceeds in this manner until all the reds have been potted. Then the colours must be potted in ascending order of value, from yellow to black. The final disappearance of the black, leaving only the cue ball on the table, marks the end of the game save when the scores are level. In this instance the black is re-spotted and the players toss a coin for choice of first shot with the Cue ball placed anywhere.

Foul strokes

The other means Of accumulating points is through your opponent's foul strokes. Failure to strike a red incurs a penalty of four points, unless the cue ball strikes a ball of higher value than that, in which case the penalty is the value of that ball. Failure to strike the nominated colour also brings a penalty of four points, except where the colour is of higher value, in which case again the penalty is that value.

If in failing to hit a low-value colour the cue ball hits a high-value colour he is penalized at the higher value Going in-off costs four points, more if it results from a shot on one of the high-value colours.

All these fouls, and consequent penalties, can be attributed to mistakes, or carelessness, but an important aspect of the game is the deliberate laying of snookers leaving your opponent in such a position that he has no direct line of play to a ball he must hit. He is then forced either to swerve the cue ball or play it off one or more cushions en route to the object ball. Depending upon the difficulty of the snooker he may well miss, may probably miss or may almost certainly miss. As well as giving you between four and seven penalty points, this can be of great tactical significance.

Should a player find himself snookered on the reds following a foul shot by his opponent, he may nominate any colour as a red. This is called a 'free ball'. If he pots it he scores one, as though it were a red, and then he chooses a colour in the normal way. If there are no reds remaining, the free ball has the value of the lowest value colour on the table, and if he pots it he must proceed with the colours in sequence, in the normal way.

In addition to those described so far, the following are all fouls:

1 Playing with both feet off the floor.

2 Playing before all the balls have come to rest.

3 Double striking on the cue ball

4 Touching the cue ball with anything other than the cue tip.

5 Playing with the balls wrongly spotted.

6 Jumping the cue ball over any other ball.

7 Knocking any ball off the table.

Complicated rules

Most of the confusions about the rules of snooker occur because the rules were laid down on the assumption that the game would invariably be refereed. The referee envisaged was not just a friend of the two players, acting like a scorer in a game of darts, but a properly qualified certificated referee. He would understand thoroughly every particular of the rules, and his application of them would be accepted in a sporting spirit. Under such circumstances, individual players could take as much or as little interest in the more complicated rules as they wished. They would merely have to comply.

The realities of snooker-playing contrast starkly with this. The vast majority of games are unrefereed, necessarily so, and always will be. In some cases this makes it impossible, practically speaking, to enforce the rules. For example, you might touch the cue ball with an article of clothing and be quite unaware of the fact, and therefore unable to call the foul against yourself. You would consider your opponent to have an unsporting attitude if he watched you like a hawk every time you addressed the ball, on the off chance of spotting such a misdemeanour. And if he did so, you might dispute it hotly. Then who would judge?

For the rest, the fact that you will be playing without a referee, except possibly on occasion, means that you really must get to grips with the rules. And you must hope to play against opponents who understand them too, because controversies stemming from ignorance will spoil the enjoyment of a game. There follow some typical examples of the practical application of the rules of snooker.

Re-spotting the balls

A long as there remain reds on she table, it is a foul to play a stroke with a colour missing. It does not matter whether it was you, or your opponent, or even a referee who failed to re-spot the missing colour. Nor does it matter when the oversight occurred. The moment it comes to light, whoever notices it, the player who has just played is adjudged to have fouled, and to have fouled at that moment. In other words, should it be discovered in the course of a break, all strokes prior to that, and therefore the score accumulated to that last stroke, are considered good. It is also a foul stroke to play when a colour has been re-spotted on the wrong spot. Again, the penalty is applied against the player in play when the mistake is discovered, even if it was not he who incorrectly re-spotted the ball.

When the spots are covered

In the course of a game it is common for one of the spots to become covered, or partially covered, by another ball. If a colour cannot be re-spotted cleanly on its own spot, it is re-spotted on the highest value spot unoccupied. If all the spots are occupied, it is placed as near its own spot as possible, without touching another ball, and in a direct line with the nearest point of the top cushion. Take the blue, for example. It would be placed as near as possible to its spot without touching another ball, between that and the pink spot and in a direct line with the pink and black spots.

A snooker

Most players think they understand well enough what a snooker is, and for the most part that knowledge is sufficient, although it is likely to be incomplete. It is generally reckoned that you are snookered if you cannot hit both sides of the ball 'on'. Strictly speaking, this is not the case. If it were, you would be snookered when breaking off, because you cannot hit both sides of any red in the triangle. You are in fact snookered when a ball not ,on' prevents you from hitting both sides of the ball 'on'. You cannot, of course, be snookered by another ball on'. That is, you cannot be snookered on a red by a red. You are snookered even if you can hit enough of the ball 'on' to pot it. Under those circumstances, the fact that you are technically snookered may not concern you, but it becomes important if such a situation arises after a foul stroke by your opponent. You may take on the pot, or you may opt for a free ball. If you take on the pot, you have waived your right to a free ball. You cannot, say, hit the intervening ball and claim it retroactively as a free ball. If you nominate a free ball you must not only hit it before hitting any other ball, you must not lay a snooker behind it. If you do, you have fouled. This is an important rule because it prevents you from trickling the cue ball up behind a free ball to snooker your opponent. You are, of course, entitled to play off the free ball so as to snooker your opponent behind another ball. And you are entitled to use the free ball to help you pot a ball that is 'on', for instance as a plant, as long as you hit the free ball first.

The touching ball

Nothing in snooker causes as much confusion as the touching ball rule. One aspect of it appears at first glance to be contradictory, and so it will always seem until you fix it firmly in your mind. First, the uncontradictory aspect of the rule. The cue ball must be played away from the ball it is touching without disturbing it. Otherwise it is a foul.

Now to the confusing bit. If the cue ball is touching a ball that is 'on , whether red or colour, then in the act of playing away from it a player is deemed to have played it, He may send the cue ball where he likes, without touching another ball, and he has played a lawful stroke. If, on the other hand, the cue ball is touching a ball that is not 'on' (either red or colour), then in the act of playing away from it he is deemed not to have played it, because otherwise it would be a foul stroke. He is obliged to hit a ball that is 'on', or it is a foul stroke.

Suppose you are touching a red and on a red. You can play away from the touching red to pot another red, or to lay a snooker elsewhere on the table, wit or without hitting any other ball. If there are no reds left and you are touching the yellow and 'on' the yellow you must attempt a safety shot, preferably a snooker, because there is no ball for you to pot. You would automatically foul by disturbing the yellow unless you initially played away and struck it via a cushion. In a situation where the reds are gone, the colours all remaining and you are touching the black, you must hit the yellow, even if you are snookered on it.

The last two colours

It is obviously the intention of the rules to ensure that a player can never gain an advantage over his opponent by fouling. If he could, it would lead to deliberate fouling, which would change the nature of the game in an unthinkable direction. There is one particular instance in which the free ball rule, as explained so far, could give rise to just that. Only pink and black remain on the table, your opponent has just fouled, but even with the penalty forfeit you are still more than thirteen points behind and therefore require a snooker to win. In the course of fouling, he has snookered you on the pink, thereby giving you a free ball. What are you to do? You must nominate the black, and if the black happens to be in a good potting position all is well, because it would be re-spotted after you pot it. If not, you are in deep trouble because the free ball rule prevents you from laying a snooker behind the black. You must simply play it safe. Worse, suppose the pink is in an easy potting position. Your opponent has you at his mercy, and all because of the outcome of that foul stroke. To remedy that defect in the free ball rule, it has been altered to exempt this unique situation from it. When only pink and black remain, it is permissible for a player to lay a snooker behind the black.

Miscellaneous points

1 There is a popular misconception that the game is not properly underway until the cue ball disturbs the pack of reds. Should the player making the first stroke miss the pack entirely, he thinks that he must play the shot again from the 'U. This is entirely wrong. The game begins the moment the cue tip strikes the cue ball on the opening shot. Missing the reds is a foul with the appropriate penalty. It is now the next player's turn to play on the reds and if he is snookered the free ball rule is applied, even at this stage.

2 If a ball is forced on to a cushion rail, runs along it and then drops back on to the table, all is well. If it is an I on' ball and it runs right along the cushion rail to drop into the pocket, it counts as a good pot. If it remains on the cushion rail it is a foul, just as though it had been forced right off the table. The penalty is either its own value or the value of the ball 'on', whichever is the higher. If it is a red, it is put in a pocket, as it would be if it were knocked off the table. If it is a colour it is re-spotted.

3 Occasionally, a ball may hover tantalizingly on the edge of a pocket before falling in. If it does so only momentarily, it is counted as in. If, however, it falls in later, without being touched, it is replaced on the edge of the pocket. If it falls in during the course of a shot, the balls involved are all replaced and the shot is taken again, without penalty.

The 'Professional Rule'

There can be many instances in a game in which a player could gain an advantage through fouling, despite giving away the requisite number of points. There is a rule prohibiting an intentional miss on a ball 'on', but this not only requires a referee to adjudge, it also poses a terrible dilemma. Was it a deliberate miss or just a rotten shot? Was he cheating or was he simply lucky to gain an advantage from an incompetent shot? This is not the only type of foul that could result in injury to the innocent party. Suppose with only pink and black left, a player goes in-off and, by some weird but by no means impossible fluke, leaves the black hanging over the pocket with the pink so close to it that by moving the pink his opponent is bound to pot the black. That fluke result of a foul would decide the game in favour of its perpetrator.

Many years ago, the professionals decided to take this element of luck and potential controversy out of their game by adding an additional rule the so-called 'Professional Rule' as it was then known. You see it applied all the time on television and it has long since been added to the official rules. It is a rule of beautiful simplicity. It states that following a foul stroke, the next player has the right to make his opponent play again. It does not matter what type of foul stroke it was, or what stage the game is at. It has no effect whatever on the free ball rule. But just as a foul can leave you unsnookered but in a nasty position, so it can leave you with a free ball that is of no use to you. It can leave you with a shot you would find difficult to play in such a way as to achieve safety. In such a case, you apply the 'Professional Rule' and ask your opponent to take the shot.

INDEX